ENGLISH

Fast Forward

Second Edition

Lynda Berish

Sandra Thibaudeau

Collège Marie-Victorin

Prentice Hall Allyn and Bacon Canada
Scarborough, Ontario

Canadian Cataloguing in Publication Data

Berish, Lynda, date–
  English fast forward 3

2nd ed.
ISBN 0-13-082268-X

1. English language—Textbooks for second language learners.*
I. Thibaudeau, Sandra, date–   . II. Title.

PE1128.B484 1999   428.2'4   C99-930600-6

Prentice-Hall, Inc., Upper Saddle River, New Jersey
Prentice-Hall International (UK) Limited, London
Prentice-Hall of Australia, Pty. Ltd., Sydney
Prentice-Hall Hispanoamericana, S.A., Mexico City
Prentice-Hall of India Private Limited, New Delhi
Prentice-Hall of Japan, Inc., Tokyo
Simon & Schuster of Southeast Asia Private Limited, Singapore
Editora Prentice-Hall do Brasil Ltda., Rio de Janeiro

ISBN 0-13-082268-X

VP/Editorial director: Laura Pearson
Director of softside marketing: Tim Collins
ESL sales supervisor: Julie Wade
Developmental editor: Marta Tomins
Production editor: Elynor Kagan
Production coordinator: Wendy Moran
Design: Monica Kompter
Page layout: Joseph Chin
Photo research: Susan Wallace-Cox

 2 3 4 5 6 7 8 9 0 HLN 0 5 4 3 2
082268   CM12

We would like to give special thanks to Sandra Koop, Sandra Roscanu and Richard Goldman for their support. We'd also like to thank Sandra Koop for testing the material in this book and Max Goldman for proofreading the manuscript.

Contents

To the Teacher

The *English Fast Forward* Series

The *English Fast Forward* series is designed for young adults learning English for work, career, or college-education purposes. It is a dynamic blend of imaginative interactive activities. Whole-language and grammar activities are treated thematically with the interests of college-age students in mind.

English Fast Forward 3 is aimed at students who already have a good command of basic English structures and vocabulary, but who need to develop their ability to cope with more sophisticated demands in the form of richer language use. The book will help these students develop greater accuracy and depth in their language production and understanding.

The Activities

The second edition of *English Fast Forward 3* incorporates many suggestions from teachers, and has been thoroughly classroom tested. New themes are based on up-to-date topics that students want to talk about. The addition of CBC video and audio clips provides further stimulation for student interaction. Many of the video and audio segments come from CBC programs such as "Out Front" and "Undercurrents," which are produced by or geared towards college students. Many of the new readings come from web sites of particular interest to teenagers and are written by college students.

The twelve units in the book have varied formats. Each consists of one or two challenging readings and a listening passage, as well as grammar, video, and speaking activities. A wide variety of activities accompany the listening and reading passages. The eight new video clips provide visual stimulation. New speaking activities encourage students to speak for longer lengths of time. The "Grammar Close-Up" sections provide innovative grammar practice in each unit. Three units feature "Where to Find Friends," a section on "Gallicisms" that sometimes create difficulties for students at this level.

Teacher's Manual

A complete teacher's manual accompanies the book. The manual contains instructions for the activities, suggestions for getting the most out of each unit, and a complete answer key. Tape scripts for the listening passages are also included.

Achievement Tests

A new set of reproducible mid-term and final exams are provided in the teacher's manual. These exams follow the format and themes of the book, and test for listening, reading, and writing. There are also suggestions for testing and evaluating oral production.

The authors wish success and satisfaction to their colleagues and to the students who use these materials.

Lynda Berish
Sandra Thibaudeau

UNIT 1

You're Smarter Than You Think

Learning Objectives

In this unit you will:

- discuss education, intelligence, talents, and abilities

- listen to information about succeeding in college

- read about different kinds of intelligence

- review the present tense: simple and continuous

- watch a video about the life of a teenager

- build writing skills in paragraph organization

YOUR DAILY SMILE
If you think you can, you can.
— *Robert Louis Stevenson*

1

Non-Stop Talking

In groups of three or four, talk about these questions. Keep talking for 20 minutes. Be prepared to give the class a summary of your group's ideas and information.

1. What does it mean to be "smart"?
2. What does "talent" mean?
3. What are your special talents?
4. What do you like to do in your spare time?
5. What kinds of things would you like to learn in the future?
6. What were your favourite subjects in elementary and high school?
7. What is your favourite course now?
8. Which courses do you find the most difficult?
9. Which courses are the most useful to you?
10. Which courses do you think will help you most in the future?
11. What are some similarities between high school and college?
12. What are the differences between high school and college?
13. What do you like best so far about college?
14. Does anything about college worry you?
15. Do you think you will work harder in college than you did in high school?
16. What kinds of activities do you participate in at college?
17. Is it easy to make friends in college? Why or why not?
18. Is English difficult for you? Why or why not?
19. What kinds of activities would you like to do in your English class?
20. What jobs or careers interest you?

Brain Power

Work with a partner. Solve as many puzzles or problems as you can in ten minutes.

A. How many hexagons are on page 3?

How many triangles are created by the overlaps?

How many diamonds are created by the overlaps?

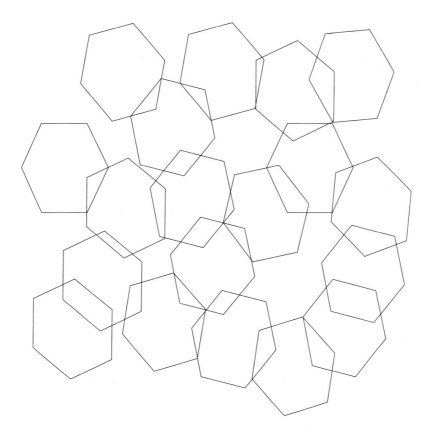

B.   During college registration, the fire alarm rang. Some students left their forms on the table and ran out. Now the secretary can't remember who wanted which course. She can only remember what the students were wearing. Help the secretary match the students with the courses.

1.   Alain was wearing a red sweater.

2.   Maria was signing up for a math course.

3.   The student who wanted philosophy wasn't wearing a yellow sweater.

4.   The student with the green sweater was registering for history.

5.   Richard was not wearing a yellow sweater.

6.   Melanie was wearing a blue sweater, not a black one.

7.   Chantal was registering for chemistry. She was not wearing yellow.

8.   The student with the blue sweater was registering for Spanish.

	Alain	Maria	Richard	Melanie	Chantal
course					
sweater					

C.   For each word on the list, think of as many songs as you can that include that word.

1.   love

3.   happy

2.   blue

4.   baby

D.   Find a solution.

You have just moved into your first apartment. You live with a roommate. You really like your roommate, but lately this person has developed some habits that really annoy you. For example, your roommate is leaving dirty clothes all over the apartment and eating all the food that you buy without replacing it. What do you do?

How did you do? Did you find all the answers? If you didn't, don't worry! People have different kinds of smarts. Read on to find out more about yours.

How Smart Are You?

A.   Discuss these questions.

1.   What is an IQ test?

2.   What does it measure?

3.   Do you think an IQ test is a good measure of intelligence?

4.   In what other ways can intelligence be measured?

B.   Work with a partner. Read the paragraphs and choose the best word in each set of parentheses.

How smart are you? If your answer to this (**1.** idea, question, thought) is based on some old report card or IQ (**2.** test, exam, competition), you might be selling (**3.** ourselves, herself, yourself) short. Experts have pooh-poohed the IQ test and (**4.** another, other, others) school-related tests as a true measure of (**5.** athletics, games, intelligence) and learning ability in the real world. "Smart" (**6.** are, is, was) being able to respond (**7.** happily, successfully, correctly) to new situations and to learn from past (**8.** lives, courses, experiences).

We can all learn, (**9.** so, but, and) we learn in (**10.** different, similar, other) ways. Some people learn (**11.** less, far, more) easily through books or numbers. Others learn better through interacting (**12.** for, with, by) people. There are several kinds of smart, according to educators. Being intelligent takes in any one—or more—of (**13.** it, them, him). Tuning in to (**14.** your, her, his) own kinds of smart can guide your choice of career and recreation—or simply give you a means to make any kind of (**15.** active, course, learning) possible.

Putting Your Smarts to Work

A. Prepare to Read

Forget the bad report cards and mediocre IQ test results. Intelligence comes in many forms. For example, you may be "people smart" or "picture smart." Find out which categories you score in, and how to put your smarts to work.

Read the sentences. If the information applies to you, circle the letter at the end of the sentence.

1. I'm into at least one sport or regular physical activity. **C**
2. I often see clear images when I close my eyes. **B**
3. I have a pleasant singing voice or play an instrument. **D**
4. I have opinions that set me apart from the crowd. **E**
5. I can imagine how something might look from a bird's-eye view. **B**
6. I prefer group games over solitary recreation. **A**
7. My best ideas come to me when I'm doing something physical. **B**
8. I like getting involved in social events at work or in my community. **A**
9. I have at least three close friends. **A**
10. TV jingles or other tunes often run through my head. **D**
11. If I hear a musical selection more than twice, I can usually hum or sing it back fairly accurately. **D**
12. I like to draw or doodle. **B**
13. I have a hobby or interest that I keep pretty much to myself. **E**
14. I regularly spend time alone thinking or reflecting. **E**
15. I really like working with my hands. **C**
16. I consider myself well coordinated. **C**
17. I'd prefer to spend a weekend alone in a cabin in the woods than at a resort with lots of people. **E**
18. I can easily figure out the moods, habits, and thoughts of other people. **A**
19. I find it tough to sit still for long periods of time. **C**
20. I like jigsaw puzzles, mazes, and other visual puzzles. **B**
21. I can tell when a musical note is off-key. **D**
22. I can easily tap out the beat to a piece of music. **D**
23. People often come to me for advice. **A**
24. I'm sensitive to colour. **B**

Which letters did you circle three or more times? You probably have smarts in those areas. For example, if you circled the "A" after sentences 6, 8, and 9, you have skills in the "people smart" area.

B. Read for Content

Read about the categories that apply to you. *Note:* Most people will find themselves in more than one category.

A. People Smart

Ask It, Talk It, Share It

If you are the person everyone comes to for advice, you have "interpersonal intelligence." Being "people smart" means you are quick at understanding what makes others tick. You are sympathetic and sensitive to people's moods, and you give good advice.

You learn well by talking things over with others. You also need their input in order to make sense of things. Julie, a university student, recalls that

YOU'RE SMARTER THAN YOU THINK

Susan Hirshorn

when she couldn't understand what was going on at lectures, she talked to different people and discovered that she wasn't the only one who was lost. Then she found a study partner, and together they sorted the information out. This really paid off at exam time when she was stuck on a question. Suddenly she'd remember that was exactly what she'd discussed with her study partner, and the answer would come back as clear as a bell! When learning with others isn't possible, try this:

- Treat books, tapes, and other learning materials like people. Talk to the author on a first-name basis: "OK, Dave, let's see what you're trying to say here" or "Tell me, Annie, do I have this straight?" Don't wait until you've read the whole chap-

ter to do this, advises Julie. Talking out each point or section will really help the learning sink in.
- Teach, or even pretend-teach, what you've been learning. Teach to a dog, a cat, or a snoring friend! Many educators say that the best way to find out if you really know something is to teach it.

If you have good interpersonal skills, you enjoy being with others, and work well in groups. You might consider a career as a teacher, politician, social worker, or publicist.

B. Picture Smart

See It, Draw It, Colour It

If you are "picture smart" you probably see things (in your mind and in the outside world) that others miss. But too many ideas conveyed in words or numbers may confuse you.

- Take advantage of the visual aids around you: illustrated books, how-to TV shows, computer-aided design programs.
- Try "mapping out" complex ideas on a single sheet of paper. When studying a particular chapter, Karen draws a series of circles (representing each thought or idea) with interconnecting lines to show the relationships among them. Use circles, sketches, pyramids—whatever seems to work. It's important to see the subject or problem as a whole rather than trying to understand it through bits of information.
- Colour-code information (using highlighters or tabs) in order to sort it out or remember it. For example,

a figure-skating coach uses bright colours worn on different parts of the body to help students and coaches concentrate on specific movements.

As a visual person, you appreciate art and like to create. Artistic people do well in careers in the arts, architecture, engineering, decorating, and fashion design.

C. Body Smart

Touch It, Make It, Do It

If you have body smarts, you use your body skilfully. You may be graceful or athletic. Use your talented fingers and other "body smarts" to cultivate the powers of the mind.

- Use models and other objects to think creatively. Got a problem at work? Make the stapler your "boss," the telephone your "assignment," and so on.
- Learn "in motion." For Richard, that means studying during a long, brisk walk. He carries cue cards (containing key words, statements, or math formulas) that hang from a big key ring so that he can flip through them easily.
- If your best ideas come while you're bathing, jogging, or washing the floor, try keeping a tape recorder with you to log your inspirations before they fade.
- Learn by doing. Ask if you can participate in a demonstration of your employer's product. At school, volunteer for lab work or a field trip to experience how something works.

If you have body smarts, you may be thinking about a career as an athlete or dancer. But you can also use your fine muscle control to excel at anything from fixing cars and electrical wires to brain surgery.

D. Music Smart

Hear It, Hum It, Sing It

People with musical smarts can rarely keep this to themselves. And why should you? The world would be a much poorer place without music. Now, think about using this ability to ease you through something boring or difficult.

- Make up a song or chant about something in order to remember it.
- During lectures and other aural experiences, focus more on listening than on taking notes. Whenever possible, try learning from tapes or radio.
- Experiment with different types of music to soothe your nerves or to rev you into action. Hands-on tasks (like cooking or sewing) are a real chore for many people unless they are singing along to something on the radio.

If you are musical, you may play an instrument, sing in a band, or write music. You may be thinking of a career as musician, songwriter, or singer. But even if your career isn't headed for the stage, you can use music to enrich your life and that of others. For example, you might enjoy teaching music or just singing with your friends or family.

E.   Self Smart

Sense It, Think It, Feel It

Being "self smart" means you probably learn better by listening to your inner voice. Don't confuse this with being "selfish." While selfish people seem to think about themselves a lot, "self smart" people really know themselves, and use that knowledge constructively.

- Keep a journal. Draw a line down the middle of each page. On one side, jot down the fact or concept you're trying to learn; on the other, note what it means to you: some past experience, a dream, or simply an emotion it conjures up.
- Meditate. If you don't want to be tied to the printed word, meditation is one of the easiest and most direct routes to self-knowledge. You can try focusing on a candle flame, reciting a mantra, or simply observing your thoughts. Meditation provides a means of looking at inner experiences that are often ignored in the course of people's busy daily existence. For Tara, meditation is just a good way to calm down. The calmer she is, the more confident she feels about her skills, and the easier it is for her to learn.

People who are "self smart" make good social workers and therapists. Actors and actresses are often very interpersonally insightful, and use their own emotions to create characters on stage or in the movies.

C.   Wrap It Up

Introduce yourself to someone you don't know in the class. Talk about your own kind of "smarts." Then find out about your partner's "smarts."

Succeeding at College
LISTENING ACTIVITY 1
Interview with a College Instructor

A.   Prepare to Listen

When you start college, you may be unsure of what you need to do to succeed. Read these "warning" signs now, and discuss them with the teacher. Make a note in your agenda to read them again in week 12. If all, or most of them apply to you, you are in danger of **succeeding** in college. You may never need to see a counsellor, get extra help, or repeat a course!

Six "warning signs" that you'll succeed at college:

1.   You regularly go to class, and even have your homework done.

2.   You know when papers are due and when exams are scheduled.

3.   You persist in getting help when you don't understand something.

4.   Teachers know you because you regularly participate in class.

5.   You never miss exams or important assignments unless you are sick.

6.   You find enjoyment in your courses and your college experience.

All these signs apply to English class as well. But there are a few special ones to add.

Six "warning signs" you'll **succeed** in English class:

1. You speak English in class, even when others lapse into French.

2. You have a marked tendency to sit at the front or middle of the class, not at the sides or in the back row. You regularly participate in class.

3. You watch movies or TV in English and even read an English newspaper or magazine occasionally.

4. You continue to come to English class even when you have many assignments due in other courses.

5. You recognize that English is a tool, a means of communication, that will help you in the future.

6. You look at English class as a place to interact with other students and discuss topics that interest you.

B. Listen for Information

First read the questions. Then listen to the interview and answer the questions.

1. How are schedules in college different from schedules in high school?

   _____

2. What other differences do students notice when they begin college?

   _____

3. What do students have to learn to be responsible about?

   _____

4. What three pieces of information do students get from course outlines?

   _____

5. What can students do to organize all this information?

   _____

6. Give two examples of how students can find time to study and still have fun at college.

   _____

7. What is an important ingredient of success?

   _____

8. What kind of courses should students take to increase their chances of succeeding?

   _____

9. Why should students be careful not to get bad marks or fail courses?

   _____

10. What should students do if they really don't like a course?

   _____

Grammar Close-Up

The Present Tense: Simple and Continuous

Simple Present

Use the simple present tense for:

1. Factual statements

EXAMPLES: Ice **is** slippery.

Some people **have** musical talent.

2. Habitual actions

EXAMPLES: Successful students **usually study** hard.

Colleges **don't give** degrees in November.

!

Always put an **s** on the third person form in an affirmative sentence.

Never put an **s** on the third person form in a negative sentence.

Change the auxiliary verb **do** to **does** for the third person singular negative.

A. Correct the form of the verbs in bold type. Then prepare for dictation by studying the paragraph.

Everyone **have** some talent. Some people **knows** how to sing or dance. My brother is a visual person who **like** to create. My sister isn't good at artistic activities but she **play** a lot of sports. I **doesn't have** artistic or musical talent, but I **gets** along well with other people because I **listens** well. People who **don't knows** themselves well may **thinks** they aren't talented. Then one day they find they **has** some talent they **doesn't know** about.

B. Work with a partner. Change these sentences to the negative. Make sure the sentence is logical.

1. A student who studies will probably not have good marks.

2. Some people have the talent to become famous musicians.

3. My friend Alice has the self-confidence to enter the competition.

4. Some arts programs get funding from the government.

5. Some sports get very good funding.

6. If you practise a language, it's impossible to become fluent.

7. A person who knows the meaning of hard work risks failure.

8. Drawing well comes easily to everyone who tries it.

9. Sylvie wants to become a concert pianist after her studies.

don't like

10. Daniel and Paul like classical music very much.

Present Continuous

Use the present continuous for:

1. Actions that take place as we speak

EXAMPLES: Don't disturb them now. They **are studying** for an exam.

They **are not speaking** Spanish. They **are speaking** Italian.

2. Actions that continue in present time

EXAMPLES: She **is preparing** for a competition.

We **are rehearsing** for the play. It's in two weeks.

The continuous form of the verb ends with **ing**. To show time or negation, you need the auxiliary verb **be** (or **am**, **is**, **are** in the present tense). Some verbs do not have a continuous form (e.g., **know**, **like**, **mean**, **hear**, etc.).

A. Choose the correct verb and put it into the present continuous form.

study   take   think   not plan   work   practise   correct   paint
wait   not train

1. The art students _____ a mural for the lobby of the college.

2. The team _____ for the basketball game next Saturday.

3. Our English teacher_____ our tests today.

4. Albert _is not planning_ to continue in the humanities program.

5. I _am studing_ science because I want to get into a nursing program.

6. The skaters _____ at the outdoor rink because it's too cold.

7. She _____ of taking two math courses next session.

8. My friend _____ for me at the bus stop at the corner.

9. John _is working_ in the cafeteria this week.

10. My friends and I _____ a test to find out about our special talents.

B. Put the verbs without a present continuous form into the present simple tense. Put the other verbs into the correct form of the present continuous.

1. Julie __Knows__ (know) how to play the harp and the clarinet.

2. My friends _are watching_ (watch) a hockey game on TV at the moment.

3. Some people _____ (feel) shy when they meet strangers.

4. Our coach ___*is*___ (yell) at us because we aren't training hard enough.

5. Mark is going to quit gymnastics because he ___*doesn't*___ (not like) the long hours in the gym.

6. The guys who don't practise ___*don't improve*___ (not improve) their game.

7. The younger kids _____ (want) to participate in the competition too.

8. Our teacher ___*believes*___ (believe) we will pass our exams.

9. When Melanie is practising piano, her neighbour ___*hears*___ (hear) every wrong note.

10. The basketball team ___*is not trying*___ (not try) as hard as it did last year.

C. Choose the sentence that is correct.

1. a) Tony is applying to the same program every year.
    b) Tony applies to the same program every year.

2. a) They go to the swimming pool in the summer.
    b) They are going to the swimming pool in the summer.

3. a) My sister is helping out at the daycare centre this week.
    b) My sister helps out at the daycare centre this week.

4. a) Students study hard when they know there is an exam.
    b) Students are studying hard when they know there is an exam.

5. a) This morning everyone talks about the hockey game.
    b) This morning everyone is talking about the hockey game.

6. a) Sam's drawings usually make people laugh out loud.
    b) Sam's drawings are usually making people laugh out loud.

7. a) They aren't in class because they are doing a practicum at the hospital.
    b) They aren't in class because they do a practicum at the hospital.

8. a) Sometimes Steve is bringing his lunch to eat during the class.
    b) Sometimes Steve brings his lunch to eat during the class.

9. a) Some people's talents are coming out later in their lives.
    b) Some people's talents come out later in their lives.

10. a) The student in the back of the classroom is reading a magazine.
    b) The student in the back of the classroom reads a magazine.

Matt's World

VIDEO ACTIVITY 1

"Matt's World" is about Matt Thurold, a teenager who had a very difficult childhood. By the time he was a young adolescent, he was already involved in a life of crime. This story shows us how he turned his life around, and how he now faces a bright future.

Before you watch the video, look at the main ideas listed in the chart on this page and on page 14. As you watch, write details beside these ideas.

Matt's background: – *high school dropout*
                     – *fights, jail, probation*

Matt's job at the restaurant:

Matt's parents and childhood:

Bertie Vandermark's farm:

Identification with Beethoven:

Comments of music teachers:

Life in Vancouver:

One Year Later

Events in the last year:

Matt's ambitions:

What's missing:

Plans for Christmas holidays:

Projections for the future:

Write About It

A. Prepare to Write

Share your information about the video "Matt's World" with a partner.
Add information that you may have missed to your notes.

B. Focus on Paragraphs

Write a summary of the video "Matt's World." Organize your writing into
three paragraphs. Use these topics for your paragraphs.

Paragraph 1: Matt's background

Paragraph 2: How he turned his life around

Paragraph 3: Matt's life, one year later

UNIT 2

Student Life in the Fast Lane

Learning Objectives

In this unit you will:

- discuss the interests of college students, including jobs

- read about working for minimum wage and about a bicycle courier's accident

- listen to a description of how a garage was converted for music practice

- review the past tense: simple and continuous

- practise arguing for and against a subject

- build writing skills in paragraph unity

YOUR DAILY SMILE

It's not true that nice guys finish last. Nice guys are winners before the game even starts.
—*Addison Walker*

Non-Stop Talking

In groups of three or four, talk about these questions. Keep talking for 20 minutes. Be prepared to give the class a summary of your group's ideas and information.

1. What are some of the jobs that students can do after school or on weekends?

2. What are some good summer jobs for students?

3. Why do students frequently take part-time jobs?

4. What are some benefits of part-time work for students?

5. What kinds of problems can students have when they have part-time jobs?

6. Which part-time jobs are easiest to get?

7. What skills can students learn from part-time jobs?

8. Which jobs give students the best experience for future work?

9. What are some jobs students can do outdoors?

10. What are some seasonal jobs students do (during the Christmas holidays, in summer, etc.)?

11. In which part-time jobs can you earn the most money?

12. Which part-time jobs pay the least?

13. What are some jobs in which you earn minimum wage?

14. Which minimum-wage jobs are the most interesting?

15. Which jobs are the most boring?

16. For which jobs do you have to wear a uniform?

17. Did you ever have to do something you didn't want to do (e.g., cut your hair, wear an uncomfortable uniform) for a job? How did you feel about it?

18. Did you ever have a job that you really liked? Describe it.

19. Did you ever have a job that you hated? Describe it.

20. Do you work now? Why or why not?

Students at Work

A. Match the jobs with the descriptions.

1. shovel snow	a) take care of children
2. babysit	b) use a lawnmower
3. wash cars	c) work very early in the morning
4. tutor	d) prepare food for strangers
5. work as a sales clerk	e) are up to your elbows in hot water
6. cut grass	f) get tips
7. wash windows	g) use soap and a squeegee
8. cook in a restaurant	h) use rags, soap, and a bucket
9. wash dishes in a restaurant	i) manufacture something
10. work as a busboy/busgirl	j) work in a bathing suit
11. deliver newspapers	k) help someone succeed in school
12. work in a factory	l) put shirts on hangers
13. work at a dry cleaner	m) often work after a storm
14. work as a waiter/waitress	n) put objects of different colours into piles
15. rake leaves	o) carry dirty objects on a tray
16. work as a lifeguard	p) help people choose things

B. Look at the list of jobs again. Have you done any of these jobs to make extra money? Ask people in the class. Find someone for each job.

Job	Name
1. shovel snow	
2. babysit	
3. wash cars	
4. tutor	
5. work as a sales clerk	
6. cut grass	
7. wash windows	
8. cook in a restaurant	
9. wash dishes in a restaurant	
10. work as a busboy/busgirl	
11. deliver newspapers	
12. work in a factory	
13. work at a dry cleaner	
14. work as a waiter/waitress	
15. rake leaves	
16. work as a lifeguard	

Minimum Wage Hell

A. Prepare to Read

What do you think about these "on-the-job" issues? Discuss these statements in groups. Write "A" for "agree" or "D" for "disagree" **in the first column** for each statement.

	Your opinion	Authors' opinion
1. The wages paid to students for most part-time jobs are unfair.	_____	_____
2. Students generally don't mind when they have to wear uniforms at work.	_____	_____
3. It's unreasonable for students to use part of their paycheck to buy their uniforms.	_____	_____

4. Students who have visible piercings in parts of the body such as the nose or eyebrow should remove jewelry from these parts before they work with the public.   _____ _____

5. Customers in stores or supermarkets feel upset if the people serving them have a distinctive appearance (purple hair, tattoos, piercings, etc.).   _____ _____

6. The way you look or dress can affect the way you do your job.   _____ _____

7. Employees should be allowed to dress any way they like at work.   _____ _____

8. Students should do anything employers ask them to do, if they want the job.   _____ _____

B. Focus on General Ideas

Read the story quickly. See if the authors agree or disagree with the statements. Write "A" for "agree" or "D" for "disagree" **in the second column**.

MINIMUM WAGE HELL
Aisley Slattery and Val Cross

1. From bright yellow life preservers to turquoise cardigans decorated with corny cartoon figures, employees will wear almost anything to earn their coveted five bucks an hour. In nearly every fast-food chain, you'll find a polyestered teen sweating away in a uniform. It's bad enough that some companies force their workers to wear tacky uniforms, but why outfits that are impractical, uncomfortable, and humiliating?

2. Some employers go so far as to make their workers give up a portion of their meagre paycheck in order to buy their own uniforms. So far, we've got the employee spending almost more than she's earned. A good example of how employees are expected to conform is an incident in a grocery store. Susan Stensland, an employee, was told to give up a piece of her identity, a small eyebrow ring. Stensland was told to take it off before she went to work or there would be no more job. In need of money, Stensland complied.

3. In the grocery store's defence, the management argued that visible piercings suggest unsanitary standards. It added that eyebrow rings and other such jewelry make customers feel uncomfortable, as though the service is not of top quality. In fact, management often argues that they don't enforce dress codes to upset the worker, but rather for the customer's benefit. Are they suggesting that all their shoppers automatically believe physical appearance overrides personality? We hope not.

4.   And let's keep in mind that today's teens are continually exposed to tattoos, purple hair, and eccentric makeup. We've seen it all! And because of this, we are a generation that believes in acceptance and frowns on discrimination. The fact that a major business believes that appearance alters behaviour comes across as insulting and offensive to many of us. We are surrounded by equal opportunities and these actions feel like a step back in time. Such actions might be considered prejudice. Last time we looked, we were pretty sure nose rings did not alter the art of bagging groceries. In some food chains, employees must wear a bandage to cover up the piercings. Which looks more sanitary to you? An eyebrow ring or a band-aid covering what might be a wound? We suggest just letting employees wear their minuscule fashion accessories.

5. Finally, we teenagers are not naïve. We do realize that in the vast minimum wage world, there are certain reasonable rules and regulations we must follow. But this is MINIMUM WAGE, after all. We should be given comfortable uniforms that we should not have to pay for. And as for the piercing thing, we feel it shouldn't be an issue because it does not alter performance, not does it get in the way of friendly, efficient service.

C. Focus on Content

1.   How many of your opinions were the same as the points raised in the article? With a partner, discuss whether you have changed your point of view for any statement. If you have, explain why.

2.   This article come from a newspaper column called "The Ravings Chronicles" where people who have strong feelings on a particular subject write their point of view. What are the main points the authors make about each of the topics below? Write one sentence to summarize their point of view about each one.

Uniforms: _____

_____

Salary: _____

_____

Personal appearance: _____

_____

D. Focus on Language

The authors use descriptive language to state their points of view.

1.   List two colourful descriptions of uniforms teens wear (paragraph 1):

a)   _____

b)   _____

2. What does "tacky" mean (paragraph 1)? Which other three words in the sentence give more information about the authors' point of view about uniforms?

   tacky: _____   a) _____

   b) _____   c) _____

3. Find two ways of describing the money that workers earn. One of these is a positive description, the other is negative. Which is which?

   a) _____ (paragraph 1)

   b) _____ (paragraph 2)

4. Which word is used to describe how customers feel, in the view of employers (paragraph 3)? Is this a strong word?

   _____

5. What three words do the authors use to express their ideas about the attitude of businesses (paragraph 4)?

   a) _____   b) _____

   c) _____

6. What do the authors mean by a "step back in time" (paragraph 4)?

   _____

E. Internet Project

Visit the Internet site for "The Ravings Chronicles" at http://spankmag.com Look in "The Zone" or in the archives for articles that interest you. Write your own ideas about a topic you see on the site or about a related topic.

My Garage

CBC ● LISTENING ACTIVITY 2

A. Prepare to Listen

Discuss these questions.

1. Do you have something you are passionate about (sports, music, etc.)?

2. How easy or difficult is it for you to take part in this activity?

3. Is location ever a problem for you (finding space to practise, etc.)?

4. What particular problems do young musicians have?

5. Do you know anyone who is in a band? What kind of music does he or she play?

6. Where do the band members get together to practise?

B.   Listen for Information

This listening passage is from "Out Front," a radio program written and produced by teenagers. First, read the sentences below. Then, as you listen, match the sentences that describe each situation.

1.   The car couldn't fit in the garage. __d__

2.   Anna's teenage son joined a newly formed band. _____

3.   The garage was cluttered and damp. _____

4.   There was a lot of noise coming from the garage. _____

5.   Anna brought spaghetti, apple pie, and pizza. _____

6.   In summer people kept their windows open for fresh air. _____

7.   The sound police said the decibel level was too high. _____

8.   Anna's son started playing jazz. _____

9.   Anna's son has a cool jam space. _____

---

a)   The band was shut down.

b)   The guys nailed outgrown clothes to the walls.

c)   The guys thought the garage would make a good practice space.

d)   The garage was filled with garage sale finds.

e)   The garage was properly insulated for sound.

f)   The guys put carpet on the floor and put up paintings against the walls.

g)   Everything was devoured with appreciation.

h)   Some people found the noise unbearable.

i)   Anna planted vines and spruced up the outside of the garage.

The Last Call Is a Close Call

A. Prepare to Read

This story is about a student who works as a bicycle courier. From the title, predict what you think happens in this story.

B. Focus on Comprehension

Read the article on pages 23 and 24 quickly. Then work with a partner to answer these WH-information questions **orally**.

1.   **Who** is the story about?

2.   **What** is her job?

3. **How** did she get hurt?

4. **Who** helped her?

5. **What** happened in the end?

6. **Why** do you think everyone responded in the way they did?

The Last Call Is a Close Call

Warren Perley

It's the courier's version of "last call"—the rush delivery before the close of business on a Friday afternoon. Only two days on the job, 18-year-old Talia already knows the drill as her green mountain bike skirts over potholes in turbid laneways. Avoid gridlock. Drive for the light. Even if it means squeezing through an intersection where that light has turned red. But on this warm, sunny pre-Halloween afternoon, the trick won't work and there's no treat waiting for Talia as she pedals furiously to keep pace with a white car heading north on Mansfield St.

The white car enters the intersection of de Maisonneuve Blvd. on a yellow light that is about to turn red. Talia is on the left side of the car, believing it will shield her until they have both passed safely through the intersection. She is wrong.

Michel, driving west on de Maisonneuve in his banged-up black Pontiac 6000, notes that the white car has not cleared the intersection. He slows down to avoid hitting it. What he doesn't see is Talia on her bike: she hasn't kept pace with the white car. Michel's Pontiac catches the rear of Talia's bike, catapulting her a metre into the air.

It is 3:55 p.m. Hundreds of bustling business people freeze in the horror of those few seconds—Talia's lithe body is airborne.

It's like watching a slow-motion replay of the football "hit of the week" but this time it's not two superbly conditioned and padded athletes ripping into one another. It's the dull thud of mechanized steel smashing into flesh and the screech of skidding rubber on cement.

Miraculously, Talia is thrown through the air locked in the fetal position. She soars over Michel's car and lands with a thwack on her buttocks in the middle of de Maisonneuve.

Many among the business people and entrepreneurs, who moments earlier had been trying to finish their last-minute chores, now rush to her aid.

Michel, the driver of the car that hit her, jumps out. He looks young and scared.

He has dilated doe eyes. A black baseball cap covers his short hair and his face is mottled with acne. The words South Pole cover the front and left arm of his sweatshirt. He wishes he were there.

"There was nothing I could do," he tells a nearby businessman. "I wasn't going fast. I didn't see her behind the white car. I was scared that she had fallen under my car."

Among the first to reach Talia is Sandy, a student in her fourth year of medical studies. She immobilizes Talia in the upright position she landed in and asks questions, such as the date and time, to see whether she has suffered a head trauma.

But Talia is more concerned with her last batch of business deliveries than with her broken body. Her cellular telephone, which landed on the pavement a metre away, is handed to her by a nearby businessman. She asks that someone call her office and let them know that she is running late.

"You're far too concerned with your job at this moment," Sandy admonishes her in a gentle manner. "Let's take care of you."

But Talia, who has taken this job as a courier to support herself while she goes back to finish her high-school diploma at night, has one more piece of business on her mind. She looks at Michel, the driver of the car that hit her, and says: "It was my fault." Michel, 19, and clearly shaken, says softly "I hope you'll be OK."

At that moment, they both look vulnerable. Oddly, each of them is wearing running shoes with the laces undone—Michel in his Adidas and Talia in her Fila.

All of five minutes has elapsed. Despite the usual Friday rush to get things done and go home, there is no shortage of help. Two businessmen have used their cellular phones to call an ambulance. Another man in a suit has jumped into the middle of de Maisonneuve to redirect traffic.

Sandy and a businessman in a blue suit help release the straps of Talia's green backpack. Sandy persists in her questioning. Talia knows the date and time. She also knows there is a searing pain shooting from her right shoulder down to the middle of her back.

Within 10 minutes, Urgences Santé has arrived on the scene. A technician, together with Sandy, slowly remove Talia's green helmet

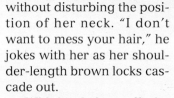

without disturbing the position of her neck. "I don't want to mess your hair," he jokes with her as her shoulder-length brown locks cascade out.

With her helmet off, she is a dead ringer for a dark-haired version of Brooke Shields—the blue eyes, the finely chiseled features. In her red and blue flannel shirt and blue sweatpants, she exudes style down to her long, gold-lacquered fingernails.

In the short space of 15 minutes, at least three others on bikes pass the scene. Seeing one of their own supine, they stop. Talia, who is speaking perfect English to Sandy, switches effortlessly to French. "Salut Luc, je suis correcte."

The Urgences Santé technician, who has been speaking English to her, asks whether she prefers that he speak to her in French. She opts for English. He asks her whether she has any medical condition he should be

aware of. "Minor asthma and a major back problem," she says with a smile.

Everyone is taken with Talia's courage, humour, and charm. The Urgences Santé technicians reassure her as they immobilize her neck with a cervical collar and apply three black straps binding her to a stretcher for the journey to hospital.

"There is a 99-percent chance that everything is all right and that you're going to go home after they check you out in the emergency department," one of them tells her. His reassuring words bring a smile.

As they lift the stretcher, she turns to Sandy and to one of the businessmen who had stayed by her side during the 20-minute ordeal. A wan smile creases her face. A barely audible "thank you" tumbles from her trembling lips. The businessman, his financial statements and Friday deadlines forgotten, has a tear in his eye.

C.   Focus on Content

Put the events of the story in the correct order. The first sentence has been done for you.

_____ Talia is on the left side of the white car.

_____ Sandy, a medical student, checks to see if Talia has a head injury.

_____ Talia asks someone to call her office.

_____ Michel's Pontiac hits the back of Talia's bike.

_____ Other couriers pass by, and stop when they see Talia.

_____ Talia flies a metre in the air and lands in the middle of de Maisonneuve.

_____ Urgences Santé arrives and removes Talia's helmet.

_____ Talia thanks the businessman who helped her while she waited for the ambulance.

__1__ Talia pedals to keep pace with a white car heading north.

_____ Urgences Santé technicians put Talia on a stretcher.

D.   Focus on Cause and Effect

Match the cause and the effect.

1. Talia stays on the left side of the white car _____

2. Michel hits Talia's bike _____

3. Hundreds of people stop in their tracks _____

4. Sandy asks Talia questions _____

5. Talia asks someone to call her office _____

6. Talia works as a courier _____

7. Talia tells the driver of the car that hit her, "It's my fault" _____

8. The Urgences Santé technicians immobilize her neck _____

9. Talia is taken to the emergency room _____

10. Talia says "Thank you" to one of the businessmen _____

---

a) because he didn't see Talia.

b) because she has pain in her shoulder and back.

c) because she's worried that she's running late.

d) because she wants to see if Talia has head injuries.

e) because Michel looks very upset.

f) because they want to check her out.

g) because he stayed with her throughout her ordeal.

h) because she believes it will protect her at the intersection.

i) because she needs to support herself while she finishes high school.

j) because they see Talia flying through the air.

Grammar Close-Up

Simple Past Tense and Past Continuous

Simple Past Tense

Use the simple past tense for actions completed in past time.

EXAMPLE: I **watched** the balloon take off.

The regular form of the simple past tense is formed by adding **ed** to the base form of the verb.

EXAMPLE: I watch   I **watched**

Many common verbs are irregular in the **affirmative form** of the simple past tense. See the chart in Appendix 2 on page 175.

A.   Review irregular past tense forms by completing the chart below.

1.	begin	_began_	24.	meet	_met_
2.	become	_became_	25.	_pay_	paid
3.	break	_broke_	26.	put	_put_
4.	_bring_	brought	27.	read	_read_
5.	_buy_	bought	28.	_ride_	rode
6.	catch	_caught_	29.	ring	_rang_
7.	choose	_chose_	30.	_run_	ran
8.	_come_	came	31.	_see_	saw
9.	drink	_drank_	32.	_sing_	sang
10.	_drive_	drove	33.	speak	_spoke_
11.	_eat_	ate	34.	stand	_stood_
12.	feel	_felt_	35.	_steal_	stole
13.	_find_	found	36.	swim	_swam_
14.	forget	_forgot_	37.	take	_took_
15.	fly	_flew_	38.	_teach_	taught
16.	_get_	got	39.	tell	_told_
17.	_give_	gave	40.	think	_thought_
18.	go	_went_	41.	_throw_	threw
19.	have	_had_	42.	understand	_understood_
20.	_hear_	heard	43.	_wake_	woke
21.	know	_knew_	44.	_wear_	wore
22.	_leave_	left	45.	win _gagner_	_won_
23.	make	_made_	46.	write	_wrote_

Negative and Question Form

Regular and irregular past tense verbs form the negative in the same way. The auxiliary verb **did** signals past time and **not** signals negation. The main verb is always in the base form. The contraction of **did not** is **didn't**.

EXAMPLES: They **saw** the accident.   They **did not see** the accident.

I **watched** the ambulance arrive.   I **didn't watch** the ambulance arrive.

To form a question, signal past time by using **did** before the subject. Use the base form of the main verb for regular and irregular verbs.

EXAMPLES: They **saw** the accident.   **Did** they **see** the accident?

They **watched** the girl.   **Did** they **watch** the girl?

!

Irregular past tense verbs are used only in the affirmative form. The negative and question forms use the base form of the verb, not the irregular form.

A.   Complete the conversation. Use the correct form of the verb. Use contractions.

Sandy: I really enjoyed that job. The boss told us such great stories.

David: He _did not_ (not tell) great stories. He _told_ (tell) boring stories.

Sandy: Well, anyway, we got paid quite well. We _learned_ (learn) a lot. And we _made_ (make) some new friends.

David: We _did not_ (not earn) much money. We _didn't_ (not learn) anything important, and we _did not_ (not make) new friends—they were just acquaintances.

Sandy: Yes, well…. We were lucky. We _worked_ (work) in a fabulous hotel for the summer. We _had_ (have) a great view of the ocean, and the sun _shined_ (shine) every day.

David: We _did not_ (not work) in a fabulous hotel. It was boring. We _did not_ (not have) a great view of the ocean. We could only see the parking lot. The sun _did not_ (not shine) that much.

Sandy: David, I'm surprised. You _had_ (have) a positive attitude this summer.

David: I _didn't_ (not have) a positive attitude. I just _wanted_ (want) to keep my job.

B.   Write ten questions in the past tense to ask someone about a job he or she had.

Past Continuous Tense

Use the **past continuous tense** to focus on an action in progress in the past. Use the **past continuous** for an action that was not finished when it was interrupted in the past.

EXAMPLES: I **was studying** until midnight last night.

I **was studying** when the phone rang.

Use the past form of the auxiliary verb **be (was, were)** to show past time. Use the ending **ing** to show continuous action.

EXAMPLE: It was raining hard yesterday.

    past   continuous

Negative

Use the **past continuous negative** to say that an action was not taking place in the past.

EXAMPLE: It **was not raining** this morning.

Use the past tense form of the auxiliary verb **be + not** for negation. Use the **ing** form of the main verb.

We were not driving too fast.

past   negation   continuous

A.   Match the questions and the answers.

1.   How did the accident happen?

2.   How did you know that the neighbours were away?

3.   Why were you surprised to see your sister here?

4.   How did you know it was cold out?

5.   Why did the store lose money?

6.   Why are these pictures so dark?

---

a)   The camera wasn't working very well.

b)   People were wearing coats and hats.

c)   She said she was spending the day at home.

d)   Their newspapers were lying on the doorstep.

e)   Nobody was shopping there anymore.

f)   The driver wasn't paying attention.

B.   Some sentences have errors. Find the errors and correct them.

1. It weren't raining before the accident happened.

2. We were having a wonderful time before the accident.

3. The bicycle courier were crossing the intersection when the car turned.

4. A witness were speaking on his cellular phone.

5. Two women was standing on the corner chatting.

6. Some people was eating on an outdoor terrace.

7. The victim wasn't lying on the ground. She was sitting.

8. The police officer was checking the driver's identity.

9. The driver of the car were sitting on the curb shaking.

10. The courier weren't smiling when the paramedics arrived.

Simple Past and Past Continuous

A.   Practise the simple past and the past continuous. Rewrite this report of Talia's accident in past time.

It is like watching a replay, but it's not two athletes who are ripping into each other. The car hits Talia and sends her flying through the air. Talia soars over the car and lands in the middle of the street. People who are eating on a nearby terrace run to help her. The driver looks young and he is wearing a baseball cap.

Talia asks someone to call her office and say that she is running late. Then she turns to the driver who is looking shaken and says that the accident is her fault. The driver and Talia are wearing the same kind of running shoes. All Talia notices, however, is the pain in her shoulder. When the ambulance arrives, Talia, who is speaking English to Sandy, switches to French. The ambulance technician tells her that she is going to be OK.

Two Sides to Every Question

Choose one of the following subjects. When the teacher calls your name, talk for one or two minutes to support **Statement A**. When the teacher says "Stop," switch to **Statement B**, and give arguments to support it. The class will decide which of your arguments is most convincing.

1.   **Statement A:** Students who work part time learn job and money-management skills.

   Statement B: Students who work part time generally waste their money, and their class work suffers.

2. **Statement A:** Students who work with the public shouldn't dye their hair strange colours or have body piercings.

   Statement B: Students should be allowed to express their individuality and dress as they please, even on the job.

3. **Statement A:** Minimum wage is fair and reasonable for most part-time jobs.

   Statement B: Even for part-time jobs, students should make good wages. They generally work very hard at their jobs.

4. **Statement A:** Uniforms are part of the job. You shouldn't complain if you have to wear one.

   Statement B: People shouldn't be forced to wear uniforms that are uncomfortable or unattractive.

Write About It

Focus on Paragraph Unity

1. Work in groups to discuss the following the topic: "Should students work part time?" Think of reasons for and against part-time work for students. List the reasons.

2. Write two paragraphs about the topic, one for and one against working part time.

UNIT 3

Getting Kids Off the Streets

Learning Objectives

In this unit you will:

- discuss street kids and petty crime

- read about a program to get kids off the streets

- watch a video about street kids

- build skills in choosing topic sentences

- learn how to use "will" and "be going to" to express future time

- listen to an interview with a sports coach

YOUR DAILY SMILE
Things do not change. We change.
—*Henry David Thoreau*

Non-Stop Talking

In groups of three or four, talk about these questions. Keep talking for 20 minutes. Be prepared to give the class a summary of your group's ideas and information.

1. Do you ever see teenagers living on the streets? Where?
2. Why do you think people end up on the streets?
3. How do street kids stay alive?
4. Do you think it's a good idea for kids to wash windshields for money?
5. What programs or facilities should be available to help street kids?
6. What are street kids' biggest problems?
7. Why do some teenagers turn to crime?
8. At what age are teenagers most likely to turn to crime?
9. What kinds of crimes do teenagers commit?
10. What is a good punishment for petty crimes (e.g., writing graffiti)?
11. What kind of role models do teenagers need?
12. Name some people that teenagers admire (athletes, rock stars, etc.).
13. Why do some teenagers join gangs?
14. Is there anything positive about gangs?
15. What kinds of skills do street kids need in order to get jobs?
16. What are the biggest problems teenagers face?
17. Do you think teenagers feel optimistic or pessimistic about the future?
18. How are teenagers today the same as, or different from, their parents when they were teens?
19. What are the best things about being a teenager today?
20. What advice would you give a younger brother or sister about growing up?

Midnight Basketball

A. Focus on Main Ideas

Read the story quickly for the main ideas. Then answer these questions **orally** with a partner.

1. **What** is midnight basketball?
2. **Where** does it take place?
3. **Who** takes part in the program?
4. **Why** did Van Standifer think the program was necessary?
5. **How** will this program help street kids?

Midnight Basketball

James Christie
and Robert MacLeod

Toronto—A plan to offer young men in Canadian inner cities the opportunity to stop running with the wrong crowd in exchange for running with a basketball crowd is being explored by government and sports administrators. The program is called Midnight Basketball and it's a creative attempt to get youth in high-crime areas off the street and give them not only basketball but some lessons in life skills.

The Ontario Basketball Association hopes to implement programs in Toronto as early as this spring. "The program caters to the inner city athletes across the province and across the country," says the OBA. "We're talking about a group of kids who aren't generally doing anything positive at that time of day. If they're not at home, they're in the streets, doing something that's not positive, and that's why Midnight Basketball is being offered."

Canada's late-night hoops will be based on a successful prototype established in the United States, which is now offered to some 10 000 young adults in 50 US cities. The $6-million Canadian project is directed to areas where there are suitable locations to initiate the program, to give oth-erwise idle young men between the ages of 18 and 24 something to do.

"An important ingredient of the Midnight Basketball concept is mandatory life-skills programs that would be offered to participants in exchange for the opportunity to play some hoops. The programs would be taught just before the games themselves. Games would begin late in the evening and continue until after midnight.

The aim is to get kids off the street and into something positive and to use basketball as a vehicle to teach life skills as well. Some athletes won't buy into it, but those who don't won't be around for long. Eventually, the 500 athletes who do buy into it will go to classes," said the director.

"Once we get them focused on something, we can use basketball as the vehicle to teach them about staying in school, and how to get and keep a job. Teaching is a large component of this." Basketball is not the only factor. It's an enhancer of social skills as much as basketball skills.

It will be at minimal cost or no cost to the participants. If the program proves successful, consideration would be made to expand it into Montreal, Vancouver, Edmonton, Halifax and possibly Winnipeg.

The concept of Midnight Basketball was initially envisioned by a man known as G. Van Standifer. Although Van Standifer refused to give his first name, he used to enjoy telling people that the G stood for "Get them off the streets." The national director of the association said that Van Standifer was struck by how much crime in the community was being carried out by young male adults.

"He realized that the answer was not just trying to arrest them as fast as you possibly could," he said. "He thought if there was just one way that he could either get them to think about what they were doing or get them out of harm's way just for a moment, that it might help.

"He thought about basketball for the simple reason that it was so popular with the younger crowd. And because it is an activity that can be played at night indoors, he felt if he could get some of the gyms that were closed at night to open and get these people off the street, it might help."

He organized workshops for the players where they would be instructed in such areas as finding a job, improving education, and birth control methods. If the players didn't make the workshops, they couldn't play.

The first summer that the program was offered, the crime rate among the targeted youth was reduced by almost 60 per cent within the community. A program consultant with Youth Service Canada went to Chicago in December to scout the Midnight Basketball leagues that have operated in that city since 1989. Currently there are four leagues with 32 teams.

Killings carried out by street gangs are not uncommon in Chicago and officials there say it is not uncommon to have representatives from four or five rival gangs playing in the league at the same time. The organizers approached the gang leaders to seek assurances that the gangs "would agree not to kill each other for the next 10 to 20 weeks" so that the basketball program could be run. So far, the games have gone off without a hitch.

B. Focus on Details

Find **three** correct ways to complete each sentence.

1. Midnight basketball is

   a) ___ a way for government and sports administrators to play basketball.

   b) ___ a way to get young adults in trouble with the law off the streets.

   c) ___ a way to teach young adults life skills.

   d) ___ a plan for downtown Toronto only.

   e) ___ based on a successful program in the United States.

2. An important part of the program is

   a) ___ teaching young adults life skills.

   b) ___ using basketball to teach students how to stay in school.

   c) ___ having basketball games available from morning to evening.

   d) ___ making students pay for the program.

   e) ___ showing students how to get and keep a job.

3. G. Van Standifer says

   a) ___ the best way to get kids off the streets is to arrest them as soon as possible.

   b) ___ a lot of crime in the community is committed by young male adults.

   c) ___ if he could get young adults to think about what they're doing, it might help.

   d) ___ basketball could help because it's popular with young adults.

   e) ___ one problem was that many people didn't like to play indoors.

4. The midnight basketball program

   a) ___ organized workshops for the players, which they were required to attend.

   b) ___ reduced the crime rate by 60 percent the first summer it was introduced.

   c) ___ can have members of four or five rival gangs playing together.

   d) ___ had one killing of a gang leader in Chicago.

   e) ___ had a lot of problems when the games began.

C. Focus on Language

Match the words or phrases with similar meanings.

   1. inner cities ___   a) won't agree (to participate)

   2. caters to (inner city athletes) ___ b) an original model

   3. hoops___   c) with nothing to do

   4. a prototype ___   d) first thought of

   5. idle (young men) ____   e) safe

   6. mandatory (program) ____   f) a way

   7. a vehicle ___   g) with no problems

   8. won't buy into it ____   h) the people it's designed for

   9. enhances (social skills) ____   i) noticed

  10. initially envisioned ____   j) basketball

  11. was struck by ____   k) obligatory

  12. out of harm's way ____   l) helps increase

  13. the targeted youth ____   m) downtown cores

  14. without a hitch ____   n) is designed for

Sandra's Kids

CBC ⦿ VIDEO ACTIVITY 2

This video segment is about a unique woman named Sandra, who dedicates her life to helping street kids.

A. Listen for Information

To prepare for the video, read the questions. Then, as you listen, answer the questions with short answers. **Write only the key words.** Don't try to write full sentences.

1. Who are the staff in Sandra's store?

    _____

2. Name some businesses Sandra sets up.

    _____ _____

3. What happens to the money that the store makes?

    _____

4. Why did Sandra quit her day job?

    _____

5. What kind of job skills does Sandra teach the kids?

    _____

6. What does Toby do every day?

    _____

7. How has Anthony's attitude changed?

    _____

8. How does Sandra help when kids have to go to court?

    _____

9. What two jobs does Gypsy do?

    _____

10. What do the kids say about Sandra?

    _____

11. What is the payoff for Sandra?

    _____

B. Focus on Language

These are some expressions from the video. What do these expressions mean?

1. a neat store
    a) an interesting store
    b) a store where it's easy to find things
    c) a store that's clean

2. (Toby is learning to) stretch a looney
    a) make more money
    b) use his money in the best way possible
    c) find a way to spend his money

3. ...give them a break
    a) ask them for information
    b) ask them for help
    c) help them with a problem

4. petty crime
    a) small crimes
    b) crimes by young adults
    c) major crimes

5. ...a sentiment shared by the kids
    a) all the kids are very sentimental
    b) all the kids are sensitive
    c) all the kids feel the same way about it

6. The payoff comes at the end of the day.
    a) Everyone gets paid at the end of the day.
    b) Nobody gets paid very much at the end of the day.
    c) People see the benefits of their work later on.

7. cover the overhead
    a) make sure the roof is fixed
    b) pay for regular expenses
    c) pay for occasional expenses

Skill Building

Focus on Topic Sentences

A.   Look at these facts from the video. Put them into the correct categories.

	About Sandra	About street kids	How Sandra helps
Toby cooks meals for 20 people.		✔	
Sandra goes to court with the kids.			
Sandra has a two-year old.			
Anthony wants to get his own apartment.			
Sandra gets leases on stores.			
Sandra teaches the kids how to manage money.			
Sandra helps more kids than the politicians do.			
Sandra used to be a real-estate agent.			
Sandra quit her job to help street kids.			
Sandra taught Gypsy how to repair bikes.			
Anthony feels more grown up now.			
The kids learn how to pay the bills.			

B.   Choose the best topic sentence for each paragraph.

Paragraph 1: About Sandra

a)   Sandra is a special person who devotes her life to helping street kids.

b)   Sandra used to be a real estate agent before she started to help street kids.

c)   Sandra is an amazing person who does all kinds of special things.

Paragraph 2: About the street kids

a)   Some street kids work in bike-repair shops or other stores.

b)   Kids who used to live on the street are learning job skills for the future.

c)   Anthony and Tony are two street kids who are doing better now.

Paragraph 3: How Sandra helps

a)   Sandra teaches the kids to write cheques and to pay their bills.

b)   Sandra helps kids by standing up for them in court.

c)   Sandra offers many practical solutions for the kids.

Grammar Close-Up

"Will" and "Be going to" to Express Future Time

"Will"

Use **will** + the base form of the main verb for:

1.   saying what someone is willing to do in future time.

EXAMPLE: The coach **will hold** tryouts at three tomorrow.

2.   predictions related to what we personally believe will happen in future.

EXAMPLE: We **will win** if we practise hard.

3.   formal announcements of future events.

EXAMPLE: Tomorrow's game **will begin** at eight o'clock.

Negative Form

Use **will not** + the base form of the main verb for negation in future time. In spoken English, the negative contraction **won't** is generally used.

EXAMPLES: The players **won't make** that mistake again.

We **won't win** if we don't work harder.

Late arrival at practices **won't be** tolerated.

A.   Complete the sentences with the affirmative or negative form of **will**, based on information from the article "Midnight Basketball."

1.   A life-skills program _____ **be** offered in exchange for an opportunity to play some hoops.

2.   Young men who join the program _____ **stop** running with the wrong crowd.

3.   Athletes who don't follow the rules _____ **be** around for long.

4.   The 500 athletes who join the program _____ **go** to life-skills classes.

5.   Unfortunately, some street kids _____ **find out** about the program in time to sign up this season.

6.   The Ontario Basketball Association _____ **implement** the program in the spring.

7.   Midnight basketball is played in a gym. It _____ **be played** outside.

8.   The program _____ **cost** the sponsors $6 million dollars the first year.

9.   There _____ **be** any cost to Midnight Basketball participants.

10. Kids from rival gangs _____ **be excluded** from participation in the league.

11. Players who don't make the workshops _____ **play** in the games.

12. Kids who play basketball at night _____ **be out** committing crimes.

"Be going to"

Use **be going to** + the base form of the main verb for:

1.   predictions that result from present events.

EXAMPLE: The players are on the court. The game **is going to** start.

2.   statements of intention related to plans or decisions.

EXAMPLE: They **are going to** play the national anthem before the game.

In spoken English, the contraction is generally used for the auxiliary verb.

A.   Use the information in the first sentence as background information. Use the information in brackets to make predictions about the future. Use the correct form of **be going to**. Use contractions.

EXAMPLE: Tony has good experience working in Sandra's restaurant.
(get a job easily).

He's going to get a job easily.

1. A lot of players attend the workshops. (learn useful life-skills)

2. Mike is running with the wrong crowd. (get into trouble)

3. Midnight Basketball programs are effective. (reduce the crime rate)

4. Sandra gives kids a chance to run the store. (find out how to manage money)

5. Anthony has a new job managing the bike shop. (rent his own apartment)

6. Tanya knows how to cook for a crowd. (feed 20 people tonight.)

7. Sandra's help gave me self-confidence. (look for a job in a store)

8. Those guys have picked up a lot of life-skills. (have successful lives)

9. Those boys love to play sports. (join the Midnight Basketball program)

10. The program is successful in many cities. (expand to other cities)

B.   Use the information in brackets and make the sentences negative using **not be going to**. Use contractions.

EXAMPLE: Jack is wasting his time in class. (pass the course)

He **isn't going to** pass the course.

1. Some kids refuse to attend the life-skills course. (be allowed to play)

2. That kid is busy with courses and basketball at night. (be able to commit crimes)

3. Tom has his own apartment now. (live on the streets anymore)

4. Municipal governments are worried about juvenile crime. (ignore the problem)

5. I have learned how to manage money. (have problems making ends meet.)

6. Jane knows that winter is coming. (continue to live on the street)

7. Sandra's program for street kids is famous. (have trouble getting financing for it)

8. Toby learned a lot about fixing bikes. (be without a job for long)

9. We have a new gym in the neighbourhood. (play ball in the streets anymore)

10. Joe made some new friends at Sandra's store. (feel lonely like he did before)

Something for Everyone

LISTENING ACTIVITY 3

Interview with a Sports Coach

A. Prepare to Listen

Discuss these questions.

1. What are some benefits of participating in team sports?

2. What role does the coach have in a team sport?

B. Listen for Information

Listen to the interview and answer the questions.

1. Name some sports that Richard plays.

_____

2. Why did Richard begin coaching?

_____

3. What does he like about coaching?

_____

4.   What was special about Richard's water-polo team?

   _____

5.   How benefits did Richard get out of competing?

   _____

6.   What does Richard suggest for someone who wants to become
     involved in sports?

   _____

Write About It

Focus on Topic Sentences and Supporting Details

Write a three-paragraph composition entitled "Helping Street Kids." Use
information from this unit as well as your own ideas. Use the outline form
below.

1.   Write three topic sentences in the chart.

2.   List supporting details (examples, statistics, descriptions, reasons).

3.   Develop your paragraphs.

Topic sentences	Supporting Details
_____	_____
	_____
	_____
	_____
_____	_____
	_____
	_____
	_____
_____	_____
	_____
	_____

The Hype Over Hemp

Learning Objectives

In this unit you will:

- read about the legalization of hemp and its uses

- listen to an interview with a hemp farmer

- practise distinguishing between fact and opinion

- build skills in choosing and writing topic sentences

- learn about question formation with "be" and "do" as auxiliaries

YOUR DAILY SMILE

A smile is the shortest distance between two people.
—*Victor Borge*

Non-Stop Talking

In groups of three or four, talk about these questions. Keep talking for 20 minutes. Be prepared to give the class a summary of your group's ideas and information.

1. What is hemp?

2. What kind of hemp products do you know about?

3. Where can you get hemp products?

4. Can you get high on hemp?

5. What is the Latin name for hemp?

6. Is it legal to grow hemp in Canada?

7. What are hemp's nutritional benefits?

8. What is hemp's relationship to marijuana?

9. What are the effects of smoking marijuana?

10. Can smoking marijuana lead to the use of other drugs?

11. Does marijuana have any medicinal effects?

12. What is the penalty for possessing marijuana in Canada?

13. In which parts of the world is the penalty for possession of marijuana most severe?

14. In which parts of the world is marijuana decriminalized?

15. Should marijuana be legalized? Explain your answer.

16. Is drug use on the rise or on the decline in today's society?

17. How easy or difficult is it to get drugs on the streets?

18. Should drugs such as cocaine or heroine be controlled by the government? Explain why or why not.

19. Which of the following causes the most problems to society: drugs, alcohol, or tobacco? Explain why.

20. Should alcohol or tobacco be declared illegal? Explain your answer.

Hoopla Over Hemp

A. Prepare to Read

What do you know about hemp? Do this quiz in groups. Choose the correct answers.

1. Which is **not** true about hemp?
    a) It's the same as marijuana.
    b) It has no hallucinogenic properties.
    c) It is high in protein.

2. What is "Cannabis sativa"?
    a) the Greek name for hemp
    b) the Latin name for hemp
    c) the Latin name for LSD

3. Which of these is true about hemp?
    a) It was the world's largest agricultural crop until the late nineteenth century.
    b) Hemp has never been grown in Canada.
    c) It is illegal as an agricultural crop in Canada.

4. Hemp and marijuana plants:
    a) are difficult to distinguish from each other.
    b) look very different from each other in colour and shape.
    c) are very different in size.

5. Hemp is a good crop to grow because:
    a) it grows very slowly.
    b) it doesn't deplete the earth of nutrients.
    c) it looks and smells beautiful.

6. For which of these things can hemp be used?
    a) paper and clothing
    b) beer and wine
    c) cosmetics
    d) all of the above

7. How much THC, the chemical that causes a "high," does hemp have?
    a) almost the same as marijuana
    b) slightly less than marijuana
    c) less than 1 percent

8. The Body Shop decided to use hemp because:
    a) hemp seed oil is a good moisturizer.
    b) they were looking for a product that appealed to men.
    c) hemp seed oil is quite expensive and unique.

B.   Focus on Content

Read the article quickly to check your answers.

Hoopla Over Hemp

Monique Polak

Montrealers are buzzing about the Body Shop's recently launched line of hemp skin-care products. "I came downtown specially to buy the hand cream," said Nadine White, 19, who was interviewed as she left the chain's Ste. Catherine St. branch, bag of purchases in hand.

What isn't quite clear is whether consumers like White are being drawn by hemp seed oil's purported moisturizing properties—or whether they're attracted by the connection to hemp's not-so-distant cousin, marijuana.

"The soap is too beautiful to use," said White, showing the hemp leaf emblazoned on the bar of soap that she'd purchased. Asked whether she'd ever tried marijuana, the CEGEP student only chuckled in reply. Her dad, Yves, 48, who had accompanied his daughter downtown, was a little more forthcoming. "The hemp boom reminds me of the sixties when I was Nadine's age. Let's just say it reminds me of another part of my life," he said.

And although Body Shop officials are going out of their way to distinguish hemp from marijuana, pointing out that hemp has no hallucinogenic property, the company's advertising campaign seems nevertheless to be capitalizing on the connection. Slogans for the new line of products include "High on Hemp," "High in protein, essential fatty acids and hysterics," and "It's Hope Not Dope."

Russ Kruta, a 20-something artist visiting Montreal from Long Island, N.Y., admitted that he doesn't usually frequent skin-care boutiques. But, attracted by the photo of a giant hemp leaf in the store's window, he decided to check out the Body Shop. "I knew they weren't selling pot. After all, this isn't Amsterdam. But I'm a firm believer in the industrial use of hemp, and I have on occasion smoked pot," Kruta said.

Carmen Sauvé, a 51-year-old resident of Hull, was spending a weekend in Montreal with daughters Natalie, 29, and Roxanne, 26. All three women loaded up on Body Shop hemp products, between them, spending close to $50—before taxes.

"I heard so much about it, I just had to try it," Roxanne said. Her mother, too, has been hearing—and reading—about the hoopla over hemp. "Besides, I'm older, and the marijuana leaf makes me feel like I'm being wild," she admitted.

The Body Shop's hemp products made news across the country this month when Health Canada threatened to forbid the chain from displaying the merchandise. "I felt like I was in a Kafka novel," said Margot Franssen, president of The Body Shop Canada. Franssen was spending the weekend at her Lake Simcoe Cottage, recovering from a bad cold brought on by a harrowing week of meetings and press conferences.

What Franssen called a "mixup" with Health Canada officials was straightened out, and the Body Shop stores began selling the hemp products on Oct. 8. "Health Canada wondered whether continued use of our products—along with drinking and eating hemp products produced by other manufacturers—could lead to a high," Franssen explained.

Hemp products have been selling briskly at the Body Shop's Ste. Catherine St. Location. "So far, the hand cream is our best seller; it's selling out quickly," reported store manager Chantal Houle.

According to the Body Shop's slick promotional brochure, the much maligned hemp plant, Cannabis sativa, was the world's largest agricultural crop from 1000 BC until the late nineteenth century. In Canada, hemp was first grown in Nova Scotia in the early seventeenth century.

In 1938, the Canadian government banned the growing of hemp, and it was only in March that the health minister agreed to allow industrial grade hemp to be grown in Canada for commercial purposes.

"In the past, the government may have worried that people might have tried to grow marijuana along with the hemp," Franssen said. But, she added, it's easy to distinguish hemp from it's illegal cousin. "The hemp plant grows to be almost 5 metres tall; the marijuana plant grows to under 2 metres," she said.

A crop that can be grown every 100 days, hemp needs little fertilizer and does not deplete the soil of essential nutrients. Versatile, it has a wide variety of industrial uses ranging from paper and clothing to beer, wine—and cosmetics. Though Franssen explained that the first batch of hemp used by the Body Shop was grown in France, subsequent batches were expected to come from southern Ontario.

Like marijuana, hemp is a member of the mulberry fam-

ily, but whereas marijuana has high levels of THC or delta-9 tetrahydrocannabinol—the chemical that causes a "high" or psychoactive effect in the nervous system—hemp has levels of less than one per cent THC.

Franssen said that the Body Shop decided to use hemp both because it is environmentally sound and because hemp seed oil is rich in essential fatty acids. "The body needs these in order to have moisturized skin," Franssen said.

Which explains why the Body Shop has come up with a line of hemp products designed to appeal to individuals—both men and women—with dry skin. Products include a hand cream, a multi-use oil that can be used in the bath, on the body or for massage, as

well as a lip conditioner and a product playfully named "elbow grease" and packaged in an oil can reminiscent of the one carried by the Tin Man in The Wizard of Oz.

Franssen believes that the public—as well as the government—needs to be educated about hemp.

"Suggesting that hemp products with hemp leaves on them will promote drug smoking is like saying that selling poppy seed muffins is going to promote heroin use," she said.

And though all the commotion over hemp has left Franssen a little sniffly, she won't deny that the controversy is good for business. "All this publicity has been great for us, but it's even better for the hemp farmers," she said.

C.   Focus on Language

Find the correct word to complete each sentence.

banned   psychoactive   briskly   harrowing   distinguish   deplete
chuckled   forthcoming   loaded up   slogans

1. Some people are very shy when they talk about themselves. Others are more _____.

2. The store was trying to _____ hemp from marijuana.

3. Some products were very popular, and were selling _____.

4. _____ for the new products in the store were displayed prominently.

5. Some products were _____ because of their connection to drugs.

6. When asked whether he had ever used marijuana, one man only _____ in reply.

7. The sales manager was feeling a lot of stress after a _____ week of press conferences.

8. People _____ on the products because they were on sale.

9. Some plants _____ the soil of nutrients.

10. Some drugs or chemicals cause a _____ effect on the nervous system.

D.   Focus on Fact and Opinion

Read the sentences with a partner and write "F" for "Fact" or "O" for "Opinion."

1. People who use hemp products are attracted by its connection to marijuana. _____

2. Hemp is high in protein and essential fatty acids. _____

3. Using hemp products makes older people feel young again. _____

4. People use hemp products because they want to get high. _____

5. The hemp plant was the world's largest agricultural product for many years. _____

6. Many people might have grown marijuana along with the hemp plant if it were allowed. _____

7. The hemp plant grows much taller than the marijuana plant. _____

8. The hemp plant is the most versatile plant of all. _____

9. Hemp seed oil is a better moisturizer than other kinds of oils. _____

10. People who use hemp products will soon use other drugs. _____

Is It Rope or Dope?

CBC LISTENING ACTIVITY 4

A. Prepare to Listen

In groups, read these questions. Answer any questions you can from your own knowledge or from the reading. Write "T" for "True" or "F" for "False."

1. Vern Mitchell was one of the first people in 60 years to grow hemp legally in Canada. _____

2. Industrial hemp can make you high if you smoke it. _____

3. Mr. Mitchell decided to grow hemp because potatoes were banned in that region. _____

4. Mr. Mitchell doesn't think hemp is a very good crop to grow. _____

5. The grain from hemp is very high in protein. _____

6. The THC level in commercial hemp is quite high. _____

7. Mr. Mitchell thinks people planned to mix his hemp with high grade marijuana. _____

8. More than 80 groups came to visit Mr. Mitchell's farm. _____

9. The problems started around September 7. _____

10. The thieves thought there was a lot of THC in the hemp seeds. _____

11. Mr. Mitchell's concern was losing money as a result of the theft. _____

12. The thieves were mostly over 18 years old. _____

13. Many other farmers had the same problems as Vern Mitchell had. _____

14. Destroying the crop was more costly than planting it. _____

15. Mr. Mitchell had to make sure the seeds couldn't grow again. _____

16. The police charged people with possession and trafficking. _____

17. The government says plants with a THC level of over .05 must be destroyed. _____

18. Mr. Mitchell plans to grow more hemp next year. _____

B. Listen for Information

Listen to the interview and check to see if your answers were correct.

C. Write About It

Write a summary of the listening passage.

Skill Building

Focus on Topic Sentences

Read the four paragraphs below. Then complete these tasks.

1. Choose the best topic sentence for Paragraph A.
    a) Marijuana used to be taxed by the government and people stopped growing hemp.
    b) Hemp has been used for a very long time in many parts of the world.

2. Choose the best topic sentence for Paragraph B.
    a) Hemp and marijuana are not the same, but they are closely related.
    b) If you smoked hemp, you would cough a lot.

3. Write topic sentences for Paragraphs C and D.

All About Hemp

A Hemp has been used in China for over 5000 years. The Chinese have used hemp for ropes and fish nets since 4500 BC, and were the first people to create paper from hemp. Hemp was also used in North America at the beginning of the twentieth century, but after the Great Depression, it was lumped together with its cousin, marijuana. The Marijuana Tax Act in 1937 put a very high tax on growing hemp, and most farmers stopped growing the crop.

B Both hemp and marijuana come from the same species of plant, Cannabis sativa. The difference between them comes from the way the plant is grown. Hemp is densely planted to produce a tall, stalky plant. Marijuana needs more sunlight and space to grow. You can't get high on hemp, because the THC content is much lower than marijuana. In fact, if you tried to smoke hemp, all you would get is a big headache, because you would have to smoke dozens of joints to feel any effects. And if you tried to smoke hemp, you would be coughing quite a bit, because hemp is so coarse it is almost impossible to inhale.

C _____

All the parts of the hemp plant can be used. Hemp oils and seeds are highly nutritious, and are purported to have healing properties. The oils are also used in products ranging from moisturizers to inks. The flower can be added to produce delicious perfumes and powders. The stalk can be used to make fibre for textiles, paper, clothing, and building materials. For example, hemp fibre is used to make jackets, knapsacks, upholstery fabrics, quilts, notepads, parachutes, baseball caps—the list goes on.

D _____

By using hemp for paper, we can cut down on the destruction of forests and preserve natural habitats. And hemp is good for the soil because it doesn't need much fertilizer, and it actually replenishes the soil rather than depleting it of nutrients.

Also, many fuels can be made from hemp, to reduce the amount of pollution from other gases and oils. Hemp can benefit people economically, too. Now that the demand for tobacco is dropping off, farmers can use their land to cultivate hemp.

Where to Find Friends

Good Friends (If You Spell Them Right!)

Some words have the same meaning in English and French, but they are spelled differently, and can get you into trouble when you write.

Work with a partner to test your knowledge. Partner B: Turn to page 54.

Partner A

Ask your partner to spell these words in English. Then write the English words your partner dictates.

apartment	problem	government
courier	aid	reasonable
object	company	human
future	class	courses
horror	progress	visit
interview	musicians	season

Grammar Close-Up

Question Formation with "Be" and "Do" as Auxiliaries

"Be" With the Continuous Aspect

The continuous aspect is formed with the auxiliary verb **be** + the present participle of the main verb. The question form puts the auxiliary verb **be** at the beginning of the sentence.

EXAMPLES: **Is** he talking? **Are** they listening?

A.   Use the information from the article "Hoopla Over Hemp" to write ten questions using the present continuous form.

"Do" With the Simple Aspect

Use the auxiliary **do** or **does** to form questions in the simple aspect.

Example: **Do** you use hemp soap?

A.   Make questions from the following statements.

Hemp soap **dries** your skin. **Does** hemp soap **dry** your skin?

1.   Farmers in British Columbia grow hemp.   *do*
2.   Hemp needs only a little bit of fertilizer to grow well.   *does hemp need*
3.   Hemp has a high level of THC.   *does Hemp have*
4.   Some stores decide to market hemp products.   *do some Stores*
5.   People say that hemp is good for the environment.   *do*
6.   The Body Shop has a line of hemp products.   *does ... have*
7.   Hemp products appeal to both men and women.   *do*
8.   Products include a hand cream and bath products.

"Be" and "Do"

A.   Make questions from these statements using the correct auxiliary verb.

1.   A farmer in Victoria has trouble when he tries to grow hemp.
2.   Some farmers are quitting the hemp business because it brings problems.   *are some farmers quiting?*
3.   Hemp grows well in the climate on Vancouver Island.   *does Hem grow.*
4.   Soap made from hemp prevents dry skin.   *— does ?*
5.   People grow hemp in many parts of the world.
6.   Hemp growing is becoming popular with farmers.   *is Hemp growing be-coming*
7.   Governments support projects to grow hemp.   *do*
8.   The hemp-farming industry is spreading in popularity.   *i...*

Where to Find Friends

Partner B (from page 53)

Write the English words your partner dictates. Then ask your partner to spell the following words in English.

address	groups	recommend
dance	percent	correct
list	author	community
example	subject	partner
fault	difficult	publicity
medal	uncle	reason

UNIT 5

Making It Right

Learning Objectives

In this unit you will:

- discuss how individuals can make a difference

- read about a 12-year old boy who has made a difference and about an unusual punishment for drunk driving

- discuss appropriate punishments for various crimes

- watch a video about alternative punishments

- listen to an interview with a young man who received an unusual punishment for drunk driving

- learn about giving advice using "should" and "must"

- write to express an opinion

YOUR DAILY SMILE

We can do anything we want to do if we stick to it long enough.
—*Helen Keller*

Non-Stop Talking

In groups of three or four, talk about these questions. Keep talking for 20 minutes. Be prepared to give the class a summary of your group's ideas and information.

1. Did you ever feel angry about something and want to change it?
2. What are some things in the world that you feel are unjust?
3. Have you personally ever been the victim of an injustice?
4. Do you believe that an individual can make a difference when something is wrong?
5. What are some injustices that have attracted worldwide attention?
6. Did you ever think of joining a movement to fight for a cause you believed in?
7. Have you ever given your time as a volunteer? How?
8. Have you ever done something you felt sorry about afterwards?
9. Do you think the law provides effective punishment for people who do wrong?
10. What are some of the ways that people who make mistakes can "make things right"?
11. What is the difference between a mistake and a crime?
12. For what kind of crimes is jail an effective punishment?
13. Do you drive a car? Do you give friends rides in your car?
14. How long have you been driving?
15. Have you ever had an accident or a "close call"?
16. How would you feel if you caused an accident where someone else was injured or killed?
17. At what age do you think people have the strongest sense of injustice?
18. Which causes would you be willing to support financially or otherwise?
19. What percentage of people actually do things that make the world a better place?
20. Name some ways in which people can make the world a better place.

Changing the World at 15

A. Read for Main Ideas

Scan the article on page 57 and answer these questions.

1. Who is the story about?
2. What did he do?

Changing the World at 15
Craig Kielburger, Child Activist

Monique Dykstra

1. On April 19, 1995, in a comfortable suburb north of Toronto, 12-year-old Craig Kielburger flipped idly through the morning paper. He was looking for the comics. Instead, he found a horrifying story about a Pakistani boy. This story changed Craig's life forever.

2. At age 4, Iqbal Masih was sold into slavery by his parents for less than $16 dollars. Iqbal was shackled to a carpet loom for 12 hours a day, 6 days a week. Amazingly, his will was never broken: he escaped and began speaking out against child labour. When his story began receiving international attention, he was shot dead near his home in Lahore, Pakistan. He was 12 years old. Just like Craig Kielburger.

3. With a group of his friends, Kielburger started a human-rights organization called Free the Children. Their mission was to fight child labour exploitation. Three years ago, the head office of FTC was the Kielburger garage. Today, FTC has offices in 20 countries, more than 5000 youth members, and 15-year-old Kielburger has just finished writing his first book.

4. In *Free the Children,* he writes about the shocking variety and extent of child

labour he encountered during his travels at age 12 (without his parents), through Bangladesh, Thailand, India, Nepal and Pakistan. He was in Montreal last week promoting his book. Without a doubt, Kielburger is one of the most remarkable people I've met.

5. "Part of the reason I wrote this book was to prove youth are capable. Plain and simple. Youth are capable. That's something society doesn't believe. For example, on the cover of my book, in big letters, it says 'CRAIG KIELBURGER.' Big letters. Big photo of me. Then underneath, in tiny letters, it says 'With Kevin Major.'" Well, people automatically assume Kevin wrote this book. But he didn't. That's exactly my point.

6. "Children aren't simply empty vessels waiting to be filled: we're people with ideas, talents, opinions, and dreams. Some call young people idealists, as if it's a stage we need to outgrow. But I think the world could do with more idealists and dreamers. It was the dreamers who thought the Berlin Wall would fall; that women should have the right to vote; that apartheid in South Africa would end.

7. "Free the Children is a group of children speaking in defence of children. We have no vested interest: we're not paid, we don't run factories, we don't run for political office. There's nothing we have to gain besides simply doing good. Even the book. Every single cent—all the royalties—is going to projects that benefit children. I think that's what makes our message so pure—it comes from the heart."

For more information about FTC, visit its web site at www.freethechildren.org*

B. Focus on Content

Answer these questions with a partner.

1. Why did the newspaper story make such a big impact on Craig Kielburger?

    _____

2. What was the mission of Free the Children?

    _____

3. What did Craig hope to prove by writing this book?

    _____

4. What does Craig Kielburger cite as some accomplishments of idealists and dreamers?

    _____

5. Why does he say that children are effective advocates?

    _____

C. Focus on Language

Find these words in the article and use the context to choose the best meaning.

1. **shackled to** (paragraph 2)   a) tied to   b) seated at   c) opposite to
2. **a carpet loom** (paragraph 2)   a) a floor cover   b) a machine
    c) a factory
3. **exploitation** (paragraph 3)   a) make unfair use of   b) use in an un-usual way   c) occasionally
4. **encountered** (paragraph 4)   a) made up   b) avoided   c) witnessed
5. **underneath** (paragraph 5)   a) above   b) below   c) beside
6. **empty vessels** (paragraph 6)   a) lonely people   b) people without ideas   c) old fashioned people

D. Internet Project

Visit FTC's Internet Site at www.freethechildren.org*

Get more information about Craig and Save the Children to report on in class.

Let the Punishment Fit the Crime

A. Focus on Dictation

Read the following paragraph. Then close your book for a dictation.

Since the beginning of time, human societies have tried to find answers to questions of justice. The times we live in reflect our ideas of just and effective punishments. But what are just and effective punishments? Is it appropriate to hang a pickpocket or a murderer? Is jail a just punishment for vandalism or drunk driving? Do rich and poor people face the same justice system? Some say that how we answer these questions is the measure of who we are as a society.

B. Focus on Opinions

Work in groups to discuss appropriate punishments (e.g., fines, jail, community service, etc.) for the following crimes. What should be the objective of punishments?

shop-lifting	drunk driving	manslaughter
vandalism	murder	molesting children

Shame and Punishment

 CBC VIDEO ACTIVITY 3

Read the questions with a partner. Then watch the video and answer the questions.

1. Judge Ted Poe says that he doesn't want to see people leave the courthouse laughing at the criminal justice system. What kind of sentencing is he known for in Houston?

   _____

2. What reason does Judge Poe give for using this punishment?

   _____

3. Give examples of shaming sentences that are mentioned in the video.

   a) in Pennsylvania _____

   b) in Tennessee _____

   c) in Florida _____

4. What is the main objection Mark Copplehoff, of the American Civil Liberties Union, has to "shaming"?

   _____

5. What did 17-year-old John Cody do and how does he feel about his punishment?

   _____

6. Most shoppers who see John Cody in front of the store agree with the punishment. What are some reasons they give?

   _____

7. What two points do dissenters make ?

   a) the woman in the black dress _____

   b) the ACLU lawyer _____

8. Michael Stimple molested his 12-year-old daughter and has already served six months in prison. What are the two choices the judge offers him?

   a) _____

   b) _____

9. What does the woman probation officer say about Stimple's sentence?

   _____

10. What does Mark Mauer feel would be a more appropriate sentence for someone like Stimple?

    _____

11. What was Elizabeth Patterson's crime and how does she feel about her sentence?

    _____

12. Judge Poe feels that shaming sentences:

    a) won't work for _____

    b) work for _____

13. What does the bearded man in the red tie feel could be a serious negative side effect of shaming sentences?

    _____

14. How does Carlos Costilla feel about his sentence?

    _____

A Matter of Compassion

Focus on Content

Read the article and answer the questions that follow.

A Matter of Compassion

Ken MacQueen

Windsor, Ont.—Joe Camlis and Andrew Thompson were 19 years old when they died last July in a terrible accident on a Windsor street. The car was driven by Kevin Hollinsky, also 19, their very best friend.

They were heading home from a boys' night out at a downtown bar. Hollinsky, who'd had a few beers, was driving his 1985 Firebird too fast. They were, apparently, trying for the attention of a carful of girls when he lost control on a bad curve. Two other passengers were injured. Hollinsky wasn't physically hurt.

To this point, it was a sadly typical tragedy. It occurred in Windsor, but it happens everywhere. The mixture of teens, cars, alcohol and hormones is the stuff of parents' nightmares.

What happened next, though, is not typical at all. What happened next, in the words of a provincial court judge, "is a tribute to the capacity of the human spirit." If you can possibly imagine it, put yourself in the place of the parents and friends of these two dead young men. What would you do?

The friends and family of Joe Camlis and Andrew Thompson did the hardest thing I can imagine. They fought to save Kevin Hollinsky from going to jail. He pleaded guilty to two counts of dangerous driving causing death. The Crown, understandably, asked for a jail term of eight to 14 months, to serve as a lesson to other young drivers.

Before sentencing, the families of the young men made their own submissions. Dale Thompson, Andrew's father said, "I loved my son, but I am here today on behalf of Kevin Hollinsky.... I feel no malice toward Kevin because he happened to be driving the car that night, but rather I feel compassion for him. I have seen the suffering he has endured.... Since society demands exacting a price for Kevin's mistake, I'd like to think that the price, rather than incarceration, could be a much more constructive motion....

"We have been in contact with the Windsor Police Department about arranging a programme in conjunction with area schools. The programme would consist of Kevin, along with what's left of his car, attending schools and speaking with the students about the events of that tragic evening.... Both families have already offered to assist the Hollinskys and Kevin in his attempts to reiterate to young drivers the importance of responsible driving.

I know Andrew would want it this way. I surely do."

Mary Thompson, Andrew's mother said, "Kevin was always there for my son, especially when Andrew was declared legally blind because of an eye disease. I never hesitated once to trust Kevin to drive Andrew anywhere.... Kevin, I stand beside you with love and support. I hope you have the courage to go on and make a bad judgment turn into a positive and life-saving one."

Joseph Camlis, Joey's father said, "My son is at peace now and Kevin has got all the pain. He has to go through the rest of his life suffering.... Kevin needs to start his life over now that he lost his best friends, and I don't think that it should be done in custody. He needs us around him to help him get through."

Cindy Camlis, Joey's mother said, "On July 30, 1994, Kevin Hollinsky was sentenced to a life sentence of pain, guilt, and grief, for the loss of his two best friends....

"If he is guilty of anything, Your Honour, you could say he is guilty of being a true friend.... Guilty of loving his friends so much that no matter how difficult and painful it was, he struggled as a pallbearer to carry Joey to his final resting place....

"It was Kevin I went to for advice on how to dress Joey for his funeral—casual or in a suit? We were not sure, but we knew Kevin knew Joey so well that he would be able to tell us what he would like to be seen in.... I love Kevin as my own son.... I have found solace in knowing that after the accident, when my son probably knew that he was dying, Kevin reached into the car and held Joey's hand to reassure him."

The judge was asked to show mercy to a young man whose mistake caused the deaths of two others. He called the case "unique and exceptional." Jail would serve no purpose, he said, but public education might. Hollinsky was banned from driving for two years, placed on probation and ordered to serve 750 hours of community service. Much of it will be spent speaking to young people about his tragic failure of responsibility.

Some say the sentence is too lenient for the crime. But there is nothing easy about what happened in that courtroom, or about the sentence to be served. In listening to the "profound compassion" of the grieving families, the judge recognized an exceptional act of love and courage. He showed us the difference between punishment and justice.

1. What was the result of the accident?

    _____

2. How did the accident happen?

    _____

3. What happened to the driver of the car?

    _____

4. What did Kevin Hollinsky plead guilty to?

    _____

5. What did the Crown think was an appropriate sentence?

    _____

6. How did his friends' parents react?

    _____

7. Why did Andrew's father feel compassion for Kevin?

    _____

8. What did he suggest as punishment?

    _____

9. What act did Joey's mother say showed true friendship?

    _____

10. What advice did she ask Kevin for after Joey died?

    _____

11. What gave her solace?

    _____

12. What was Kevin Hollinsky's sentence?

    _____

Grammar Close-Up

Giving Advice Using "Should" and "Must"

"Should"

Use **should** to give advice or to express opinions. Use **should not** (**shouldn't**) to advise against doing something. Modal auxiliaries are followed by the base form of the main verb.

EXAMPLES: It's getting late. We **should leave** soon.

You look tired. You **shouldn't drive** tonight.

A.   Work with a partner. Complete the sentences **orally**, giving advice for these problems with **should** or **shouldn't**.

EXAMPLE: I suddenly feel cold. **You should put on a sweater.**

1. Frank has had three beers to drink. He ...

2. An accident just happened here. Someone ...

3. We plan to go to the pub tonight. We ...

4. Joe's brakes don't work very well. He ...

5. I feel nervous about driving with her. You ...

6. People were moved by Kevin's speech. They ...

7. The police advise against drunk driving. Nobody ...

8. Drinking and driving don't mix. People ...

9. Mike always drives carelessly. His friends ...

10. Alcohol causes many car accidents. Drivers ...

!

> After modal auxiliaries, use the base form of the verb.
>
> EXAMPLES: He **should drive.** ✔ He should drives. ✘ She should to drive. ✘
>
> She **must go.** ✔ She must goes. ✘ She must to go. ✘

B.   Some sentences have errors in the verb form. Find the errors and correct them.

1. Everyone should to wear seatbelts in a car.

2. Susan shouldn't drives over the speed limit.

3. I should take lessons before my driving test.

4. Jack should drives because he's the designated driver.

5. Nobody shouldn't drive after drinking.

6. We should all pay attention to Kevin's advice.

7. Somebody should call the police to report the accident.

8. The police should to suspend the licence of drunk drivers.

9. We should never get into a car if the driver is impaired.

10.   Everyone should to be aware of the rules of the road.

"Must"

Use **must** to give strong or urgent advice or opinions. Use the negative form **must not** (**mustn't**) to advise strongly against doing something.

EXAMPLES: It is –10 outside. You **must dress** warmly.

The brakes don't work. You **mustn't drive** that car.

A.   Complete the conversations with **must** or **mustn't**.

1. His driver's licence was suspended by the judge for one year.

    That means he _____ drive for one year.

2. John has been drinking and now he wants to drive home.

    That's dangerous. We _____ let him get into the car.

3. Kevin had an accident that killed his two best friends.

    He _____ live with that thought for the rest of his life.

4. Oh no. I just got a parking ticket.

    You _____ forget to pay it or it will cost a lot more.

5. My driver's licence will expire next month.

    Oh, really? You _____ remember to renew it.

6. We will probably have a few drinks at the party tonight.

Then, someone _____ agree not to drink, so he can drive us home.

7. I think that the judge is about to enter the courtroom.

When he does, everyone _____ stand up.

8. The parents of Kevin's friends argued against sending him to jail.

They said that he _____ be punished any more than he has been already.

9. Kevin gave a very emotional speech to the students.

He told them they _____ drink and drive, no matter what.

10. Kevin was sentenced to do community service as part of his punishment.

He _____ visit high schools and talk about his experience.

Kevin's New Life

 CBC LISTENING ACTIVITY 5

A. Prepare to Listen

Work in a group. Give your opinion about Kevin Hollinsky's punishment, based on what you read in "A Matter of Compassion."

1.   Do you think the sentence was too strict or not strict enough?

2.   What do you think the sentence accomplished?

B. Listen for Information

Work with a partner and read the questions. Then answer the questions while you listen.

1. Why did the Hollinsky family have to go to Toronto?

_____

2. What was the decision of the court?

_____

3. How did the audience in the courtroom react to the judge's decision?

_____

4. According to Mrs. Hollinsky, how did Kevin feel when he received his sentence?

_____

5. What did Kevin's psychologist suggest to the court? Why?

    _____

6. Why is Kevin still "seeing someone"?

    _____

7. Do the Hollinskys think Kevin's sentence was too harsh?

    _____

8. What does Kevin say about having given the talks?

    _____

9. What did Kevin name his son?

    _____

10. What does Courtney say about Kevin's relationship with his son?

    _____

11. How does Kevin respond to requests to talk about his experience?

    _____

12. What are some of Kevin's future plans?

    _____

13. What does the interviewer say that Kevin is an example of?

    _____

Write About It

Focus on Developing Ideas

Give your opinion about alternative punishment. Choose either the information about Kevin Hollinsky or the information from the video and write a composition of four or five paragraphs.

Before you begin to write, make an outline listing your topic sentences and supporting details. The supporting details can include examples, statistics, descriptions, and reasons.

Where to Find Friends

Faux Amis (Be Careful!)

Some words look similar in French and English or are commonly used in both languages—but the meaning might be different.

Work with a partner and try to match the meanings of these words in English.

1. to demand	a) to be present at an event
2. a vacancy	b) really, truly
3. a library	c) members of your family
4. a journal	d) something a bit naughty
5. to attend	e) a place to borrow books
6. to accept	f) a meeting with a lover
7. relatives	g) a place available for rent
8. to assist	h) your mother and father
9. sympathetic	i) a book to record your thoughts
10. sensible	j) to receive something
11. actually	k) to insist on something
12. a process	l) to help someone
13. risqué	m) practical
14. parents	n) a series of steps
15. a rendezvous	o) kind and understanding

UNIT 6

Living on the Edge

Learning Objectives

In this unit you will:

- discuss risk-taking, especially in sports

- listen to an interview with an extreme-sports enthusiast

- read about a risky adventure

- watch a video about the cost of extreme sports

- write to express an opinion, using main ideas and details

- learn about using "have to" to express obligation, and "do not have to" for lack of necessity

YOUR DAILY SMILE
If you always do what you did before, you'll always get what you got before.

Non-Stop Talking

In groups of three or four, talk about these questions. Keep talking for 20 minutes. Be prepared to give the class a summary of your group's ideas and information.

1. What sports do you play?

2. How often do you play these sports?

3. How long have you played these sports?

4. What attracted you to these particular sports?

5. What benefits do you get from your sports?

6. What special skills are needed for these sports?

7. How long does it take to learn these sports?

8. What are some costs involved in these sports?

9. To whom would you recommend these sports?

10. How much risk is involved in the sports you play?

11. What are "extreme sports"?

12. Who (which age group) participates in extreme sports?

13. Why do people choose to take risks?

14. What are some of the dangers involved in extreme sports?

15. Which risky sports do people now practise that weren't around in the past?

16. Which sports would you like to try in the future?

17. Which sports are most expensive to participate in?

18. Who should pay if someone needs to be rescued while participating in a sport (e.g., a snowboarder who gets hurt or lost on a mountain)?

19. Are there any sports you've tried that you wouldn't do again? What are they?

20. Have you ever chosen to place yourself in a risky situation? Describe what happened.

Risky Business

A. Look at the pictures. What sports do you see? Which of these would you do?

B.   Work with a partner. Choose the best words to complete the paragraphs.

Risky sports (**1.** is, have, were) never been more (**2.** expensive, famous, popular). In fact, the (**3.** fastest-, slowest-, oldest-) growing sport today is mountain climbing. (**4.** Other, Others, Another) popular sports include extreme skiing, in (**5.** that, who, which) skiers drop from high cliffs, as well as paragliding and cliff-parachuting.

Today people (**6.** even, still, yet) plan their vacations around taking risks. Adventure-travel businesses offering river (**7.** skiing, flying, rafting), ice climbing, bungee jumping, and wildlife safaris (**8.** is, has, have) become a multi-million-dollar industry.

(**9.** Who, what, when) is most likely to participate in these activities? The experts say (**10.** than, then, that) one in five people is (**11.** scared, caught, addicted) to thrill-seeking. Although the group has been made up of mostly young (**12.** males, sports, athletes) up to now, young females are participating in these sports more frequently (**13.** than, then, that) in the past. Why (**14.** do, have, are) they do it? Some mountain climbers say (**15.** we, he, they) climb to add excitement to their lives, to experience thrills, or to avoid (**16.** boredom, fears, fun). Others say they want to test (**17.** our, their, your) limits, to build self-esteem, and to gain self-knowledge. Some people are driven to take risks for reasons they don't understand (**18.** themselves, herself, ourselves). But, whether or (**19.** else, not, if) they understand it, more people today are engaged in risky business.

Taking Risks

A.   Work with a partner. Read the list together. For each activity, circle the letter that is true for you.

a) I have done this   c) I would like to try this

b) I have never done this   d) I would never try this

1. go over rapids in a boat	a	b	c	d
2. go skydiving	a	b	c	d
3. bungee jump	a	b	c	d
4. dive from a cliff	a	b	c	d
5. go scuba diving	a	b	c	d
6. go hang-gliding	a	b	c	d
7. go snowboarding	a	b	c	d
8. ski on expert slopes	a	b	c	d
9. go mountain biking	a	b	c	d
10. ski jump	a	b	c	d

B.   Check your score. Are a lot of your answers As and Cs? Then you're a high risk-taker. Are most of your answers Bs and Ds? Perhaps you should think twice before attempting Mount Everest!

Extreme Sports

CBC LISTENING ACTIVITY 6

Interview with an Extreme-Sports Enthusiast

This is an interview with Rich Hopkins, who participates in and promotes extreme sports.

Before you listen, read the information below. As you listen, match the information.

1. Examples of extreme sports include __g__

2. The common denominator of extreme sports is _____

3. The level of commitment is measured by _____

4. A definition of extreme sports is _____

5. Mainstream sports include _____

6. Extreme sports are different from mainstream sports because _____

7. Rich Hopkins' injuries include _____

8. People enjoy watching extreme sports because _____

9. Ron Simeo came up with the concept of _____

10. Rich Hopkins was the first person to _____

---

a) you rely on yourself only.

b) complete a pyrotechnic bungee jump into a lake.

c) no sane person would do this.

d) extreme sports are very visual.

e) the number of broken bones you have.

f) football, baseball, and hockey.

g) bungee jumping and aggressive in-line skating.

h) anything that gets the blood rushing.

i) thirty broken bones.

j) a one-week event of extreme sports.

The Thrill of Risk

A.   Focus on Main ideas

Read the story quickly to find the answers to these questions:

1.   What was the risk the author faced?

2.   How did he feel about the risk at the end?

3.   What explanation does he give about why people take risks?

The Thrill of Risk

Bruce Weber

1.   The one time I almost died on a bicycle ride—well, "almost" is a relative term—I was on the road from A Luoi to Hue, in central Vietnam. This was three years ago, so there was no shrapnel involved or anything. I was just a guy on a bike, alone, riding a 100-kilometre stretch of lonely road that winds through mountains eastward to the seacoast.

2.   How I got there is a long story; it is amazing where you can get to on two wheels when you're not very cautious. But in any case, some hours into the journey, the road suddenly became unrideable, the pavement giving way to dirt, then pebbly gravel and then, on a very steep pitch, to a mass of sharp, broken boulders. I had to dismount and walk, maneuvering the bike on foot, up and down hills, on potentially ankle-breaking terrain.

3.   It was mid-afternoon, and being near the equator in late January, it was above 90 degrees. I was down to a few gulps of water in a water bottle and some fig cookies that had begun to spoil, many kilometres from the nearest village. I was meeting friends in Hue, but they didn't know where I was. And it occurred to me to be frightened.

4.   This may sound strange, I know, because it is easy from the perspective of safety to scoff at danger, but I was jazzed. I don't mean thrilled or excited, but vividly alert, able to think with striking focus and clarity, filled with whatever inner strength I needed to keep panic at bay. In addition, I felt physically strong; weariness gave way, however temporarily, to vibrancy. Even though I now understand that I didn't have a clue about what I was going to do, I felt amazingly competent.

5.   This is why it doesn't even embarrass me to reveal how I got out of this pickle: after three hours of nothing on the road—no cars, pedestrians, no other bicycles, wagons or mules—a blue bus appeared over a hill, its engine grinding, and I got on. But by then I'd already had my moment of being a hero to myself. What a feeling!

6.   This is, of course, the thrill of risk, the thing adventurers talk about, the answer to the question "Why?" which is perennially posed to mountain climbers, around the world-solo-sailors, trans-Pacific balloonists and their ilk. It's the only reason bungee jumping exists. It's a great subject. Writers love it.

7.   In his book *Into the Wild*, Jon Krakauer wrote about a dangerous ascent of an icy cliff: "A trance-like state settles over you. The climb becomes a clear-eyed dream." Krakauer found himself relying, for part of his explanation at least, on his own most risk-taking

moment. "At such moments, something resembling happiness actually stirs in your chest," he wrote. Indeed, the answer to "why?" usually ends up this way—speculative, unspecific. "Why? Because it makes you feel good. You relish the focus, the intensity of the moment, the Zen bliss when it's over. It prepares you for challenges. That kind of stuff."

8.   Asked why adventurers do what they do—that is, risk their lives in pursuit of extraordinary thrills—Tim Cahill, an adventurer himself, gave the "two-kinds-of-people-in-the-world" answer.

9.   "Some people are motivated by risk, uncertainty, novelty, variety," he explained. "They thrive in ambiguous situations. They like intense experiences. They believe they can control their fate. Whatever comes up, they believe they can handle it. Mountain climbers and cops have this kind of personality."

10.   At the other end of the continuum are the "risk-adverse" people, motivated by things like certainty, predictability. They would rather have familiar experiences than novel ones. They wouldn't dream of climbing Mount Everest, or any other mountain.

11.   Most people, however, are neither one nor the other, but fall into the middle. I choose to believe that everyone has a little adventurous spirit, and that it all depends on how you choose to define it. For me, it's a bike ride, and one day three years ago in Vietnam, I pushed the envelope just enough to understand, intuitively if not intellectually, why I do it at all. It was a great moment in my life, one I couldn't plan. I was lucky that the bus had come along; I knew that. But I know now I had been lucky already. Indeed, if I had known in advance that my journey would end up with me stranded and scared, I'm not sure I would have even embarked. Having endured, however, I wouldn't trade the adventure for anything.

B.   Focus on Content

Work with a partner. Read the sentences together, and write "T" for "True" or "F" for "False" after each sentence.

1. The author describes himself as a fairly cautious person. _False_

2. The author had enough food and drink to last a while. _False_

3. The author was excited in the midst of danger. _true_

4. The author considered himself a hero for surviving his ordeal. _true_

5. Jon Krakauer felt happiness when he took risks. _true_

6. Tim Cahill feels most people act the same way when faced with risks. _False_

7. Mountain climbers and cops believe they are always in control. _true_

8. "Risk-adverse people" often seek novel experiences. _False_

9. People clearly either like or dislike taking risks. _False_

10. If the author had known what would happen, he might not have taken the journey. _____

C. Focus on Language

Choose the words or phrases with similar meanings. Use the context to help you. The paragraph number is indicated.

1. shrapnel (1)
    a) artillery shell set to explode
    b) weapons carried by soldiers

2. dismount (a bicycle) (2)
    a) get on
    b) get off

3. gulps of water (3)
    a) large swallows of water
    b) small sips of water

4. scoff at danger (4)
    a) worry about things
    b) be unconcerned

5. to keep panic at bay (4)
    a) not to panic
    b) to begin to panic

6. a trance-like state (7)
    a) feeling calm
    b) falling asleep

7. Zen bliss (7)
    a) almost a religious experience
    b) a frightening experience

8. thrive in ambiguous situations (9)
    a) do very well in uncertain situations
    b) have many problems

9. push the envelope (11)
    a) go a little farther than necessary
    b) avoid taking a risk

10. (to be) stranded (11)
    a) (to be) worried
    b) (to be) alone

Extreme Expenses

CBC ⬤ VIDEO ACTIVITY 4

First watch the complete video to get the general idea. Next, read the sentences below with a partner and discuss the vocabulary and information. Then, while you listen, check **five** correct ways to complete each sentence, according to information in the video.

1. Search-and-rescue volunteers on the West Coast

   a) ✓ risk their lives in order to save other people.

   b) ✓ rescue a girl from an icy creek.

   c) ___ don't have to rescue people very often.

   d) ✓ have seen their work double in the last five years.

   e) ✓ are the busiest search-and-rescue workers in Canada.

   f) ___ didn't find the missing girl.

   g) ___ saved the girl's life.

   h) ✓ see a lot of preventable deaths.

2. Attitudes to charging for search-and-rescue services in B.C. include

   a) ✓ suggesting fines or repayment of the rescue bill.

   b) ✓ billing up to $1000 for a rescue.

   c) ✓ opposition of the head of the Emergency Response Program.

   d) ✓ concern about how to bill a family for a failed rescue.

   e) ___ suggesting closing the search-and-rescue service down.

   f) ✓ adding a surcharge to outdoor equipment.

   g) ___ concern that costs have increased tenfold. *dix fois*

   h) ___ suggesting it's only a question of dollars and cents.

3. Some of the hazards of out-of-bounds skiing include
    a) ✓   that it is done in uncontrolled back country.
    b) ✓   the presence of unmarked cliffs and gullies.
    c) ✓   the risk of avalanches.
    d) ____   getting lost on the mountain.
    e) ✓   the fact that some people don't know they are going out of bounds.
    f) ____   hearing the sound of the avalanche.
    g) ✓   the risk of being buried under the snow.
    h) ✓   the pressure of the snow, which makes it hard for anyone covered by it to breathe.

4. Jessica Johnson and Michael Carstairs
    a) ✓   floated out of bounds on a cloud of snow.
    b) ✓   thought it was amusing to be in a small avalanche.
    c) ____   understand what death means.
    d) ✓   have a realistic attitude towards the danger of avalanches.
    e) ____   were badly injured when they fell.
    f) ✓   were found unhurt on a 180-metre cliff.
    g) ✓   took all night to be rescued.
    h) ✓   involved 26 people in their search-and-rescue operation.

5. Claire Israelson of Parks Canada
    a) ✓   heads a search-and-rescue operation in the Rockies.
    b) ✓   refers to search-and-rescue operations as "God's work."
    c) ____   expects lower admission fees at Canada's national parks next spring.
    d) ____   doesn't have to rescue professional athletes.
    e) ✓   saved an ice climber who fell and broke his leg.
    f) ____   has not saved many people in the last 20 years.
    g) ✓   has saved 300 people in the last 20 years.
    h) ✓   wants people who take chances to pay for their own rescues.

6. Companies that run heli-skiing tours
    a) ✓   ask skiers to sign waivers before they get into the helicopter.
    b) ✓   run ski expeditions 8000 feet (250 metres) above sea level in the Purcell Mountains.
    c) ____   employ guides who like to talk about the hazards.
    d) ✓   have guides who analyze the condition of the snow.
    e) ____   have guides who can always predict danger on the slopes.

f) ___✓___ won't rescue anyone who gets into trouble.

g) ___✓___ rescue their own customers who get into trouble.

h) ___✓___ charge $3000 per hour up-front to rescue other skiers in trouble.

7. At Loveland Ski Resort in Colorado, the ski patrol

a) ___✓___ trains dogs to search for people trapped in avalanches.

b) ___✓___ asks out-of-bound skiers to agree to be buried in the snow to train dogs.

c) _____ doesn't communicate with the skiers they bury.

d) ___✓___ had their lives endangered by two 13-year-old boys.

e) ___✓___ asks a snowboarder to lie in a pit with his face in the snow.

f) ___✓___ finds Adam McIntosh in 15 minutes.

g) ___✓___ is opposed by a Denver attorney for ethical reasons.

h) _____ has sent several people to jail for breaking the rules.

8. The ski patrol in California

a) ___✓___ works with state legislation to jail people for up to six months.

b) _____ has seen no change in search-and-rescue operations.

c) ___✓___ has seen search-and-rescue operations triple in five years.

d) ___✓___ has sent several people to jail for more than one night.

e) ___✓___ has seen skiers taken away in handcuffs.

f) ___✓___ is opposed by the sheriff's office.

g) ___✓___ works in cooperation with the sheriff's office.

h) _____ has stopped everyone from going out of bounds.

Write About It

Focus on Main Ideas and Supporting Details

A. Work in groups to discuss the issues raised in the video.

B. Write a four-paragraph composition on the following topic:

What should be done about the cost of extreme sports?

Paragraph 1 should define the problem.
Paragraphs 2 and 3 should discuss possible solutions.
Paragraph 4 should give your opinion.

Begin by writing an outline, with topic sentences and supporting details. Then develop your paragraphs.

Grammar Close-Up

Obligation Using "Have to"

Use **have to** to express obligation or things that it is necessary for you to do. Use **have to** or **has to** before the base form of the main verb.

EXAMPLES: You **have to** be careful if you ski out of bounds.

He **has to** avoid areas where there could be avalanches.

A.   Complete the sentences with the correct form of **have to**.

1.   Snow-boarders _____ stay inside the boundaries at ski resorts.

2.   The ski patrol _____ rescue skiers who go out of bounds.

3.   Skiers who go out of bounds _____ pay fines at some ski resorts.

4.   There _____ be a policy concerning who pays for search-and-rescue operations.

5.   The government _____ pay for expensive search-and-rescue operations.

6.   People think they _____ go out of bounds to have fun.

7.   Heli-skiers _____ sign a waiver before they get into a helicopter.

8.   Banff Park wardens _____ rescue many careless hikers every year.

9.   People who are careless in the back country often _____ be rescued.

10.   An out-of-bounds skier _____ think of the risk that is involved.

B.   Match the situations below with the observations in the box on page 81.

1.   Jessica is trapped on a cliff in the back country. _____

2.   A ski resort in Colorado is faced with problems because of reckless skiers. _____

3.   Heli-skiers run a high risk of getting caught in avalanches in the back country. _____

4.   Ice-climbers can be hit by pieces of ice that fall off the sides of cliffs. _____

5.   It can cost up to $100 000 for a search-and-rescue operation. _____

6.   Some areas are known to carry the risk of avalanches. _____

a) They have to sign waivers before getting into helicopters.

b) Skiers and snow-boarders have to avoid these areas.

c) These people have to wear helmets to protect themselves from this danger.

d) It has to develop policies to cope with their behaviour.

e) She has to be found and rescued by the volunteer ski patrol.

f) The government usually has to pay the cost of such operations.

Lack of Necessity Using "Do not have to"

Use **do not have to (don't have to)** to say that something is not necessary. For the third person singular, use **does not have to (doesn't have to)**.

Examples: People **don't have to ski** in the back country.

Fred **doesn't have to ski** out of bounds.

Unlike the verbs **must** and **mustn't**, which have opposite meanings, **have to** and **do not have to** are not opposite in meaning. **Have to** suggests obligation, but **don't have to** suggests lack of necessity.

A. Complete the sentences with the correct form of **do not have to**.

1. Jan only skis in safe zones so she _____ worry about avalanches.

2. If you stay inside the boundaries, you _____ use search-and-rescue operations.

3. Heli-skiers who get into trouble _____ pay to get rescued.

4. When the snow melts, the ski patrol _____ be on the alert for emergencies.

5. Some people are athletic, so they _____ take lessons to learn a new sport.

6. Bobby _____ warm up really well before he skies the easy slope.

7. Snow-boarders who have a lot of practice _____ worry about accidents.

8. Skiers with a guide _____ plan where they are going to ski.

9. Experienced ice-climbers _____ use search-and-rescue services very often.

10. People who stay in safe areas _____ be rescued.

"Don't have to" or "Mustn't"

A.   Compare **must not** for obligation with **don't have to** for lack of necessity. Choose **mustn't** or **don't have to**. (Look back at the explanation of **mustn't** in Unit 5 if you need to).

1.   That area is designated as out of bounds. You _____ go there.

2.   If you have a season's pass, you _____ pay to use the ski lift.

3.   Janet is an expert snow-boarder. She _____ take lessons.

4.   There is a danger of avalanches. People _____ ski there.

5.   Ice-climbing is dangerous. You _____ try it without a helmet.

6.   Anne can walk after her accident. She _____ use crutches.

7.   The rescue team is there. We _____ get in their way.

8.   Heli-skiing is very popular because you _____ use a ski lift.

9.   People in good physical condition _____ worry about falling.

10. If Mike stays in designated areas, he _____ think about avalanches.

Two Sides to Every Question

Choose one of the following subjects. When the teacher calls your name, talk for one or two minutes to support **Statement A**. When the teacher says "Stop," switch to **Statement B**, and give arguments to support it. The class will decide which of your arguments is most convincing.

1.   **Statement A:** Out-of-bounds skiing should be discouraged with fines and surcharges on equipment.
     Statement B: You can't stop skiers and snowboarders from doing what they love: seeking thrills out of bounds.

2.   **Statement A:** The government should send the bill for rescue operations to the families of victims of avalanches, if the victims were in out-of-bounds areas.
     Statement B: Families of skiers and snowboarders lost in avalanches have suffered enough and shouldn't be expected to pay for search-and-rescue costs too.

3.   **Statement A:** Heli-skiing is far too dangerous and should not be permitted.
     Statement B: Heli-skiing is safe if it is done responsibly; it is not the government's business.

4.   **Statement A:** Burying young people in the snow when they break the rules is an excellent way to teach them about the danger of skiing out-of-bounds.
     Statement B: The ski patrol should not have the power to judge and punish out-of-bounds or reckless skiers.

UNIT 7

Where's Our Money Going?

Learning Objectives

In this unit you will:

- discuss money

- listen to an interview with people who work at a lottery office

- read about fashion trends and credit cards

- learn about conditional sentences (Type II)

- improve your vocabulary by doing a crossword puzzle

- watch a video about a unique garage

- argue for and against a topic

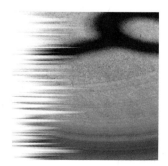

YOUR DAILY SMILE
Some people are willing to do anything for money, even work.

Non-Stop Talking

In groups of three or four, talk about these questions. Keep talking for
20 minutes. Be prepared to give the class a summary of your group's ideas
and information.

1. What are some things you regularly spend money on?

2. Where do you get your spending money (from a job, from your parents, etc.)?

3. How often do you go shopping?

4. What do you like to shop for?

5. What was the most expensive thing you ever bought for yourself? Where did you get the money?

6. Do you have a budget? Do you follow it?

7. What are the biggest money problems that students have?

8. What are some of the ways students get into debt?

9. What is the best way for students to stay out of debt?

10. Did you ever buy something and regret it later? What was it?

11. Did you ever feel you didn't get your money's worth from something you bought? What was it?

12. What percentage of your money do you spend on your clothes?

13. How often do you buy the latest trends or styles?

14. Did you ever buy an article of clothing because it was in style, even though you didn't really like? What was it?

15. If you had unlimited money, what would you spend it on?

16. Do you buy lottery tickets? Which ones?

17. Do you know anyone who won anything in the lottery? How much did they win?

18. Did you ever win anything in a lottery?

19. If you won $1 million in the lottery tomorrow, what would you do?

20. If you won $1000 in the lottery, what would you spend it on?

Big Wins

CBC   LISTENING ACTIVITY 7

When you buy a lottery ticket, you fantasize about what you would do if you won. How do you think the people who work in the lottery office feel when they hand out big prizes? This listening passage is about those people. It is taken from "Out Front," a radio show written and produced by teenagers.

First, read the questions. Then, as you listen, complete the sentences.

1. The man screams "We won. _____
   _____ ."

2. The song says "The best things _____ ."

3. Bernadette says, "The best part of the job is _____
   _____ ."

4. The busiest day is Monday because _____
   _____ .

5. The most interesting part of the job is meeting the Lotto 6/49 winners because _____ .

6. Why does Susie feel good on Mondays? _____
   _____ .

7. What record amount did the couple collect? _____ .

8. The majority of prizes are in the _____ range.

9. People come in with stories about:

   a) how they chose _____ .

   b) how they kept their tickets _____ .

10. A man kept his ticket _____ .

11. Another man taped his ticket inside the lid of his _____ .

12. The fun part is when they say, "You've _____ ."

13. People have reacted by _____ .

14. The fun part of the job is _____ .

15. The woman at the lottery office only thinks about the prize when it gets to the _____ range.

16. There are _____ staff members at the Toronto prize office.

17. _____ staff members deal with major winners only.

18. Vanaja says many lottery winners come to the office by _____ .

19. To get to the lottery office, one group of 40 members

    _____ .

20. Can employees of the lottery office play the lottery? _____ .

21. What do lottery winners do with the money?

    a) 84% of lottery winners _____ .

    b) 17% of lottery winners _____

    c) 2% of lottery winners _____ .

22. The largest cheque Bernadette ever gave out was for _____ .

23. People worry about _____ .

24. The couple who won $10 000 was so excited because _____

    _____ .

25. It's a misconception that mostly blue-collar workers play the lottery.
    In fact, it's _____ .

Trashing the Fashionphiles

A. Prepare to Read

Discuss these questions in groups.

1. How often do you buy new clothes?

2. What are the latest looks for teenagers this year?

3. Would you describe yourself as fashion-conscious? Explain why or why not.

4. How often do you change your look?

5. What influences the styles you wear (fashion magazines, movies, etc.)?

6. How would you describe your personal style?

7. Do you think people can be categorized, according to the way they dress?

8. Which of these categories do you know about? Describe them. Add any other categories of fashion followers that you know about.

    a) ravers   e) preppies

    b) skaters   f) classics

    c) hip hop/rappers   g) other _____

    d) fashion slaves

9. Do any of these categories overlap? Which ones?

10. Do you belong to any of these categories? Which ones?

B. Focus on the Main Idea

Read the article. Then decide which of these is the main idea:

a) Keeping up with new styles can be expensive and time-consuming.

b) Styles keep changing because people want to change their looks.

c) People often buy new styles just because everyone else is buying them.

Trashing the Fashionphiles

Elizabeth Bromstein

Much as I hate seeing another summer come to an end, I must admit I'm relieved I won't have to see another guy wearing a colourful sarong for at least another eight months. I'd love to meet the prankster who invented that trend. I mean, could men look any sillier? Did you see those guys walking around looking like rugby-playing harem girls? The outfit generally consisted of a T-shirt, running shoes or sandals, and a brightly patterned wraparound skirt.

Don't get me wrong, people can wear whatever they want. I just don't understand it, that's all. Maybe I have a problem with the crossing of gender boundaries, but no, wait—that's not it. I wear pants. I think what I have a problem with is stupid fashion sense—or better yet, the fashion industry in general and the sheep mentality it generates. Yes, I think that's it.

My mind boggles unfailingly at the fashion industry's ability to turn people into clones, morons, and ridiculous parodies of individuals. I guess I'll have to include myself in this one. No one is safe.

The other day I was having lunch with a friend from out of town who looked at my shoes and asked, "Do you like those?" Well, of course I like them, was my first reaction. I'm wearing them, aren't I? Then I looked at my shoes. I mean, really looked at them. They were (and I suppose they still are) running shoes with a bit of a wedge heel. Running shoes with heels. Stupid, no?

Finally, I responded, "No. I don't think I do. How'd you know?" "Easy," she said, pointing to her own chunky slip-ons. "I'm convinced I don't like these and I only bought them because I've seen so many other people wearing them and was subliminally forced into liking them."

Are we suckers? Are we pathetic followers of trends? No. Well, maybe. We simply wind up buying what's available and liking it because it's fashionable. We don't have much of a choice. Clothing is one of the few constants in most societies. You have to wear something.

Personally, I don't love clothes. I've been rotating the same four pairs of pants for two years now. I can think of a thousand other things I'd rather spend my money on and the idea of shopping leaves me cold. I hate it. So, of course, I'm a salesperson's worst nightmare, storming into shops with a "Don't try to make chitchat. Just sell me something I need and get me out of here fast!" attitude. Ultimately, I get frustrated and stalk out because nothing ever fits and everything that's fashionable nowadays is so ugly. That's how I wound up with those shoes. After a half-hour of looking,

right now. High-heeled Velcro sports sandals! Designer flip-flops with socks. (Hello, are you a Tibetan monk?) Pants big enough to camp out in. (Remember how they always used to say baggy clothes make you look fat? Well, nothing's changed.) Platforms that make us look like the Jolly Green Giant.

Do we actually believe we look good? Do we really think these things are flattering? Everyone takes it so seriously. To watch those guys in the industry talking about clothes on FT or Fashion File, you'd swear they were assessing a Modigliani, using words like fresh, free, real, deep, moody, eclectic, bold, and classic. It's just a skirt and a pair of flip-flops! Backstage, the designers are probably laughing their heads off at the suckers who are going to be wearing that stuff—us.

I know fashion is a way of fitting in and finding a niche in society. People who dress alike tend to hang out together. And it's a way of expressing your individuality, blah blah blah—even though we always wind up looking exactly like a hundred other people expressing the same individuality.

Like I have already stated, you can wear whatever you want. I know I'm not one to talk. I have purple hair. Just do this one thing for me:

Everyone who's wearing flip-flops with socks, I want

I just grabbed the cheapest ones they had in my size.

I like to look good. I just don't care about what's hot and what's not, and I'd rather do it as cheaply as possible.

A lot of people love clothes. They follow trends religiously, buy fashion magazines and get their hair cut just like their favourite television star. If there was ever an argument to combat my belief that people can take responsibility for themselves, it's in fashion.

It's amazing to watch these things unfold. One person wears something. People scoff at it. A select few (usually the young, urban avant-garde poor) start wearing it, a designer reworks it and puts it on the runway, and a year later the scoffers are wearing it too, no matter how silly it looks. Baaah!

Just look at what hip young people are wearing

you to take a good look at your feet right now and ask yourself, "Do I really like these? Would I not have collapsed into giggles if someone had walked by me wearing them five years ago?" And guys in sarongs: ask yourselves, "Am I a Polynesian princess?" If you are, fine. If you're not, put on some pants.

Trust me, you'll thank me later. Need proof? Ask your Dad about the perm he got in the '70s.

C. Focus on Content

Choose the best way to complete each sentence.

1. The author is relieved that summer is over because
   a) she prefers to wear running shoes rather than sandals.
   b) she likes the styles that guys are wearing this year.
   c) she thinks the outfits that guys are wearing look ridiculous.

2. The author thinks the fashion industry
   a) wants men and women to wear different kinds of clothes.
   b) makes people choose silly fashions.
   c) encourages people to dress as individuals.

3. The author's friend chose her shoes because
   a) she really liked the style.
   b) her friends told her to buy them.
   c) she saw so many other people wearing them.

4. The author thinks we choose our clothes
   a) to show our individuality.
   b) from what's available.
   c) because we like things that are hard to get.

5. The author's attitude towards shopping is
   a) she loves to browse in stores.
   b) she hates to shop because she hates the current styles.
   c) she likes to spend time talking to sales people.

6. She bought her shoes because
   a) she saw them in a fashion magazine.
   b) they were the only ones in her size.
   c) they were the least expensive ones in her size.

7. The author analyzes fashion trends in the following way:
   a) People who dislike something eventually end up wearing it.
   b) Most people don't like to wear designers' fashions.
   c) People generally don't wear things that look silly.

8. The author thinks the current fashions
    a) make most people look ridiculous.
    b) should be taken more seriously.
    c) are young and fresh.

9. The author says that
    a) fashion designers laugh at the people who wear their designs.
    b) most people end up looking unique and individual.
    c) people should wear what's in style.

10. The author asks people to
    a) check out the latest fashions and try to conform.
    b) ask their parents what they should wear.
    c) not follow silly fashion trends blindly.

D. Focus on Language

Which words describe fashions? Which describe people? Check the correct category.

	Fashion	People
1. colourful sarong	_____	_____
2. prankster	_____	_____
3. patterned wraparound	_____	_____
4. sheep mentality	_____	_____
5. clones	_____	_____
6. morons	_____	_____
7. wedge heel	_____	_____
8. chunky slip-ons	_____	_____
9. suckers	_____	_____
10. pathetic followers	_____	_____
11. urban avant-garde	_____	_____
12. Velcro sports sandals	_____	_____
13. designer flip-flops	_____	_____
14. platforms	_____	_____
15. scoffers	_____	_____
16. stuff	_____	_____
17. Polynesian princess	_____	_____
18. perms	_____	_____

Grammar Close-Up

Conditional Sentences (Type II)

Use a conditional sentence to show an **if/then** relationship between two actions. Use Type II conditional for present unreal—that is, hypothetical situations.

The **if** clause gives a hypothetical condition and is expressed in the simple past tense (the condition hasn't been met). The main clause that states the dream (that isn't possible) is expressed with the modal auxiliary and the base form of the main verb.

EXAMPLE: If I **won** a million dollars, I **would buy** a big house.

The meaning is that you don't have the million dollars so the house is a dream, not a reality. The whole situation is hypothetical.

The **if** clause can be first or last in the sentence with no change in meaning.

EXAMPLES: If I **had** a credit card I **would buy** a new jacket.

I **would buy** a new jacket if I **had** a credit card.

A.   Complete the sentences with things you would like to do.

1.   If I had more time to shop, I

_____

2.   If I got into debt, I

_____

3.   If someone offered me a credit card, I

_____

4.   If I thought the new styles were really ugly, I

_____

5.   If all my friends got tattoos, I

_____

6.   If I wanted to buy new clothes but I didn't have much money, I

_____

7.   If I won $500 in the lottery, I

_____

8.   If I inherited a lot of money, I

_____

B.   Complete the sentences with the correct form of the verb.

1. If I _____ (get) into debt, I would cut up my credit card.

2. He would buy new clothes if he _____ (have) enough money.

3. If I changed my mind about something I bought, I _____ (return) it to the store.

4. If all my friends bought chunky shoes, I _____ (wear) them too.

5. If my friends convinced me to change my style, I _____ (listen) to them.

6. They would invest all the money if they _____ (win) the lottery.

7. If I won a lot of money, I _____ (pay off) my student loans.

8. If she _____ (apply) for a student loan, she would get it.

9. We would save more money if we _____ (not have) so many expenses.

10. You would stay in style if you _____ (can) afford to do it.

Negative Form

Either or both clauses in a Conditional II sentence can be expressed in the negative.

EXAMPLES: If we **weren't** so broke, we **would go** on holiday to Florida.

If I **knew** more people, I **wouldn't feel** so shy.

If I **didn't like** a style, I **wouldn't** wear it.

A.   Make one or both clauses negative so that the sentences will be logical. There might be more than one correct answer.

1. I would be worried if I hadn't lost my credit card.

    _____

2. If the shoes were out of style, people would buy them.

    _____

3. If you had kept to your budget, you would be in trouble with the loan company.

    _____

4. If we didn't wear these ridiculous fashions, people would notice us.

    _____

5. We would buy the new trends if fashion designers didn't keep changing the styles.

    _____

6. If he won the lottery, he would try to borrow money all the time.

_____

7. If my friend liked weird shoes, I wouldn't buy them.

_____

8. They would win the lottery if they didn't buy a ticket.

_____

9. She would spend so much money if everything wasn't on sale.

_____

10. I would work part time if I didn't have a student loan to pay off.

_____

Question Form

To form a question with Conditional II, use the following word order in the main clause: question word + would + subject + main verb.

EXAMPLE: If you were broke, **what would you do**?

A.   Use your own ideas to complete the questions.

1. If you were a genius, what

_____?

2. Where would you look if

_____?

3. If you had the opportunity to travel, where

_____?

4. If you had all the money in the world, how

_____?

5. How would you communicate if

_____?

6. If you didn't have to work, how

_____?

7. If you had a chance to be someone else, who

_____?

8. What would you wear if

_____?

9. How would you survive if

_____?

10. If you wanted to be totally alone,

_____?

Money, Money, Money

Work with a partner to complete the puzzle. If you need help, you can turn to the glossary in Money Terms on page 100.

Across

1. A plan for managing your money is called a _____.

3. When you buy a car, you have to get _____.

4. A "P.I.N." is a personal _____ number.

8. One dollar is sometimes called a _____.

10. Some people pay cash for things. Other people buy on _____

11. The money that parents give their children is called an _____.

12. A _____ bank is often used by children to save their money.

13. To _____ money is to get money from your job.

14. Sometimes you are caught short, and you don't have enough money. You may need to _____ money from a friend.

16. If you spend too much money, you can get into _____.

20. A _____ account is useful for paying bills.

21. If you want to buy a car, you may need to take out a _____ from the bank.

22. You use a _____ account when you want to keep money in the bank for a long time.

Down

2. When you make a claim with your insurance company, you usually have to pay part of the money yourself. This is called the _____.

4. An _____ is something left to you by your parents or relatives.

5. If you keep money in the bank, you can get _____.

6. If you take out a loan, you _____ money to the bank.

7. Taking money out of the bank is a _____.

9. If you have a car accident, you have to file a _____ with your insurance company.

10. Money has two components, bills and _____.

11. Sometimes you want to buy something but you can't _____ it right away.

15. Some people buy everything they see. They like to _____ money.

17. A "grand" is equal to a _____ dollars.

18. When you buy something in a store, be sure to get a _____.

19. If you buy a lottery ticket, you can _____ money.

23. The money you receive from your job is your _____.

Get Thee Back, Plastic

A. Read the article on pages 96 and 97 for general ideas.

B. Write ten information questions about the article.

C. Exchange questions with a partner. Answer your partner's questions.

"It all started too easily" recalls Nicole, 17, of Tampa, Florida. "I got a letter from my friend at college in Miami. Could I come visit? Yeah, right! As if I had the money. Then I saw it." It was a letter from a bank offering Nicole, an unemployed high school junior, a Visa card with a $2,500 limit. "I figured, why not?" Neglecting to fill in

GET THEE BACK, PLASTIC

Margie

her age, and claiming a $4000 income, Nicole mailed back the response card. Two weeks later a different bank offered her a MasterCard. She applied for that too. In a few days, her Visa arrived. "I immediately made plane reservations. My mom asked where I was getting the money, and I told her my dad was buying me the ticket. Since they've divorced and my dad often buys me things, she accepted it." So Nicole and her buddy ate out, went to a concert, shopped like mad. When she got home, she vowed never to use the card again.

Sure. A week and a half later, her dad told her he couldn't afford the video camera he'd promised for Christmas. (She wants to be a film director and already produces and hosts a public-access TV show.) "Through my dysfunctional thought processes," she continues, "I decided I could get the camera if I used the credit card. I went down to an electronics store and purchased a state-of-the-art camcorder. Now I could shoot whenever I wanted!" On the way home she

bought a couple of CDs. Soon she was gorging on clothes, music, pricey computer accessories. "Then one day I went into a record store to get a limited edition Dinosaur Jr album. I slid over the plastic and waited patiently for the approval number. Only this time there wasn't one. I knew I had to be a lot over my limit." Nicole was really scared. Still, she promptly began charging up her new MasterCard.

Nicole steeled herself for the financial fallout by getting a job at the Gap. Meanwhile, Mom figured out that the video camera wasn't a loaner or a gift. Nicole confessed everything. Her mother was upset but tolerant; she'd had credit card trouble of her own after the divorce. Still, she told Nicole, "You bought the stuff, and you're going to pay for it."

The first Visa bill came. Nicole owed in excess of $3,000. And because she'd gone over her limit, she had to pay extra charges. Plus, all the cash advances she'd gotten from ATMs were accruing separate interest at an even higher rate. Then came the MasterCard bill—another $1,000. Nicole took a second job, in a photo shop. "Working two jobs at minimum wage put into perspective how much money is really worth," Nicole says. "I'm too tired to use my killer computer, I can barely do my TV show and I definitely don't have the time to work on the artistic films I wanted to. The music mostly had to be resold, for a huge loss, I must add."

The worst was ahead. Nicole received an acceptance letter from NYU's Tisch School for the Arts— "my dream come true," she says—but in the same envelope was the financial statement telling her the cost. "Not only was it impossible for me to make payments on the credit cards and on school, but I was not even eligible for a loan because of all the money I owed." Nicole will probably go to another school, one that offers her a scholarship. She hopes to attend NYU as a grad student—"if I can get the money together, that is," she says firmly, "because I will never be in debt again. The whole experience has left me feeling bitter. What were those companies thinking, giving a child credit cards to play with? I wasn't responsible enough to handle them, and I'm sure there are other kids in the same situation. Mainly, though, I'm angry with myself. I've always had enough control to stay away from drugs, alcohol and tobacco, but I couldn't hold back from plastic."

Students spend over $60 billion a year on consumer goods, and the Nicoles obviously don't think of the consequences. But credit card companies do. They mail applications to high school seniors, set up tables outside cafeterias, put ads in the bags at college bookstores, offer gifts and incentives if you sign up. "One company had a table during freshman week," a student recalls. "They offered a round-trip discount airfare just for signing up!" Some companies sponsor rock concerts and buy ads on college radio.

Visa and MasterCard insist they're not trying to make big bucks off you; they just want you as a loyal customer for the future (75 percent of college students keep their first card for 15 years or more). Besides, they say, college students actually default on their debts less often than the general populace. But Ruth Susswein, president of a nonprofit consumer education group says, "Many parents end up footing the bill. That's why students don't show up in the default rate. Besides, if you pay the minimum, you haven't defaulted."

Credit card companies say the vast majority of students use their cards responsibly. Still, financial experts recommend that Visa and MasterCard require students to demonstrate some ability to pay when they apply for a card, and send students a schedule showing how long it will take to clear up the average debt if they pay just the monthly minimum.

Credit cards are scary because we've all been so well trained in the art of immediate gratification. We want stuff now. Advertising tells us that with stuff comes love, popularity and success; welcome to our consumer culture. Yet on an average day, 1,500 Americans file for bankruptcy. Clearly we are deluded. And I think growing up with ATMs has helped distance us from money. They're miraculous! You push buttons and they spit bucks at you! Credit fits right into the fantasy. It is the illusion of unlimited wealth.

Now, I'm not saying you shouldn't have a credit card. They do embody peace of mind for emergencies. But it's also true that everyone is subject to "Credit Card Idiocy." Hey, I didn't understand until I started this story why I should pay off my balance in full every month. So be smarter than me, OK? Then I will feel purposeful and valid in my own right and not need to consume so damn much.

A Special Place

A. Prepare to Listen

Discuss these questions.

1. How much does it cost to buy a second-hand car?

2. What costs are involved in running a car?

3. Do you drive a car?

4. Do you feel comfortable taking your car to a garage for repairs? Why or why not?

5. Could you describe a problem with your car to a mechanic?

6. Do you think most mechanics are honest?

7. Did you ever feel cheated when you were charged a lot for car repairs?

8. What can you do if you think the mechanic overcharged you?

B. Listen for Information

This video is about a special kind of garage. Watch the video to find out what makes this garage different.

Before you listen, read the questions. As you listen, write short answers to the questions.

1. What was Sandy Spicer motivated to do?

   _____

2. What does NICs stand for?

   _____

3. What did Sandy want to do when she was younger?

   _____

4. How does the customer describe the problem in her car?

   _____

5. List three things that bug women when they get their cars repaired.

   a) _____

   b) _____

   c) _____

6. What are some features in Sandy's garage that are different from other garages?

   _____

   _____

7. How did Sandy get the idea to start NICs?

   _____

8. Name some people who work in Sandy's garage.

   _____

9. How does Sandy help women?

   _____

10. What were they worried about when Carla Morgan tried to get a job in a regular garage?

    _____

11. What does Sharon Barwick say about NICs?

    _____

12. What does Sandy feel is most important about the work she's doing?

    _____

13. What did the customer say she was happy about?

    _____

C. Write a summary of the video.

Two Sides to Every Question

Choose one of the following subjects. When the teacher calls your name, talk for one or two minutes to support **Statement A**. When the teacher says "Stop," switch to **Statement B**, and give arguments to support it. The class will decide which of your arguments is most convincing.

1. **Statement A:** Lottery winners generally spend their money wisely.
   Statement B: Most lottery winners waste their money and end up no farther ahead than before.

2. **Statement A:** Students who have credit cards learn how to budget their money.
   Statement B: Credit cards are dangerous for students, because spending can get out of control.

3. **Statement A:** Most teenagers buy clothes and accessories to express their individuality.
   Statement B: Most teenagers end up wearing the same fashions as everyone else.

4. **Statement A:** It's more important to love your job than to make a lot of money.
   Statement B: If you're making a good salary, it doesn't matter whether or not your job is interesting or useful to society.

Money Terms
A Glossary of Common Terms

afford   1. to have the money for   2. to manage to give, have, or spare

allowance   a definite portion given out to meet requirements or expenses

borrow   to get something with the understanding that it will be returned

buck   (slang) a dollar

budget   a plan for spending based on the amount of money available

cheque   written order directing the bank to pay money to the person named

claim   a demand for reimbursement according to insurance policy

coins   metal money

credit   money made available by a bank or store, to be repaid later

debt   1. the condition of owing money   2. something owed to another

deductible   money subtracted from a claim by an insurance company

earn   1. to be paid   2. to get money for work or service

a grand   (slang) a thousand dollars

identification   a means of identifying a person

inheritance   something left or given to you by a person who has died

insurance   the arrangement of payment in case of accident, loss, or death

interest   payment made for the use of money

loan   money lent with the expectation of repayment

owe   1. to have to pay   2. to be in debt for   3. to be obliged to pay for

piggy bank   pig-shaped container with a slot for coins

receipt   written statement to show that money has been received

salary   money paid at regular intervals for work

spend   1. to pay money   2. to use

win   1. to get a prize   2. gain: to get by effort, ability, success, or luck

withdraw   1. to remove, to take back   2. to take money from the bank

All About Love

Learning Objectives

In this unit you will:

- discuss love

- read about love in cyberspace and about finding the perfect person to love

- listen to a humorous discussion about pick-up lines

- learn about the present perfect for indefinite past time

- argue for and against a subject

- build writing skills in developing paragraphs

YOUR DAILY SMILE

To love and win is the best thing; to love and lose is the next best.
—*William Makepeace Thackeray*

Non-Stop Talking

In groups of three or four, talk about these questions. Keep talking for 20 minutes. Be prepared to give the class a summary of your group's ideas and information.

1. Is it possible to fall in love at first sight?

2. How do you know if you are in love?

3. What are the best ways to meet a guy/girl?

4. If you saw the girl/guy of your dreams at a party or bar, and didn't know his/her name, what would you do?

5. Should a girl ask a guy out?

6. Can guys and girls be "just friends"?

7. Have you ever done anything "crazy" when you were in love? What was it?

8. Who is more romantic, guys or girls?

9. At what age do most teens start dating?

10. Are relationships today different from when your parents were dating? Explain.

11. What are the positive and negative aspects of meeting someone on the Internet?

12. Is it possible to fall in love with someone you meet on the Internet?

13. Is there one perfect person for everyone?

14. Do you believe love is controlled by destiny?

15. Do you think people are realistic about what to expect from a relationship?

16. If you don't find true love, can you be happy with someone you really like?

17. What is most important to you in a guy or girl (looks, intelligence, etc.)?

18. Which things are not very important to you?

19. Do you know anyone who has a great relationship? What makes it great?

20. If you loved someone but your parents forbade to you see him or her, what would you do?

Cyberlove and Other Catastrophes

A. Focus on the Main Idea

Scan the story to find the main idea. What is the "catastrophe" in the story?

CYBERLOVE AND OTHER CATASTROPHES
Jessica Dzwigalski

1. They talked to each other for hours every night before they went to bed. They spent endless time together dreaming about how perfect their life was going to be. She was a college student of 19 and he was a two-time divorcee of 28. The age difference didn't seem to matter, for Pavel and Jen were in love.

2. The two were close acquaintances for nearly a year before realizing their serious feelings for each other. Not a day passed that they didn't pledge their love to each other, and hardly a night passed without shared words of passion between them. It was the classic storybook romance, complete with tentative marriage plans and dream house specs for the home they would eventually raise their family in.

3. Everything appeared perfect for the couple, except that Jen and Pavel had one thing going against them. They had never physically touched each other in real life; in fact, they had never even met in real life.

4. Jen and Pavel held their conversations in on-line chat rooms and in several nervous telephone conversations. I met Pavel several years ago in a gothic chat room and had always considered him one of my closer on-line friends. Later, when Jen joined our chatting community, we three created an immediate bond within the larger group. I have spent more hours on line in the past three years than I care to recall. After realizing the immense potential of the Internet, I swiftly became a pro Web surfer, but discovered that my true passion was inside the strange world of chat rooms. My curious mind and outgoing personality quickly entered an environment where new people were constantly appearing and diversity was the norm. Although I found it easy to accept all of my new on-line friendships, my cynical mind scoffed at the idea of an on-line romance; after all, how could you love someone you had never met?

5. I found it fascinating how easy it was for me to communicate intimately, sharing my innermost feelings and secrets with those who were essentially complete strangers, but I was skeptical of Net romances. Suddenly I was an active member in a tight-knit community, a new world where anything appeared possible. I chatted with Jen for several months before we planned "The Trip." That is how we referred to it: "The Trip." We were to meet in Chicago for a two-day gothic music festival the last weekend in July. We were both so excited, she more than I, for Pavel would be there. For the first time, the two would finally get to meet face to face.

6. I arrived at the Palmer Hilton Hotel in downtown Chicago almost 15 minutes before our pre-arranged meeting time and was nervously tapping my feet in line, waiting to check in. Suddenly I heard a female voice behind me timidly speak my name. I turned and there was a tall, black-haired young woman standing beside a small suitcase. I knew who it was right away. "Jen!" I managed to squeak out before we hugged like long-lost friends. We talked excitedly all night about what the next day would bring; we were going to meet Pavel at the first of two concerts at the Vic Theatre near Belmont.

7. After spending some of the day walking around Chicago's shopping district, we headed for both the theatre and an adventure we would never forget. The air was humid inside the theatre; it was filled with many strange and interesting creatures, all swaying to the ethereal music being played on the small stage. Jen was nervous about meeting Pavel, and we walked around the large room for several minutes before they found each other. Jen told me later in the hotel room that their eyes met, and she had known it was him. They hugged tightly, neither wanting to let go, and I discretely left the two of them alone for about ten minutes before returning to join in the conversation. I was curious as to how things were going.

8. Good thing I returned when I did. It was surreal the immense tension that was building between the two of them. They were sitting in awkward silence together, neither one making an effort to create a conversation. We made it through the show and went out for coffee afterwards. Pavel and I, who had always been friends in the chat room, hit it off and talked about many things while Jen sat across from him, unable to be as care-free with her cyber-soulmate in the real world as she had been on line.

9. I found it strange the way Jen and Pavel behaved, and believed their preconceived notions of each other (and the relationship they believed they shared) had caused them to share nothing but hurt feelings and bitter silence that weekend. The built-up personalities that formed from their on-line conversations were unattainable in real life.

10. The Internet has provided one of history's first true forums for people to meet with no preconceived, "sight-based" stereotypes. The only thing other people on line know about is what you care to share with them. This

is the Internet's most alluring characteristic, and its most dangerous imperfection. It is all too easy for people to put on different faceless "masks" in a chat-room setting. Although it is perfectly healthy and acceptable for people to vent their real-life stresses and live out their fantasies, like so many other things, they must be careful not to hurt themselves or others while participating in such fantasies.

11. Pavel and Jen and I still gather now and then to chat in our old stomping ground, although past hurt and anger between the two of them is still very apparent. And unfortunately, harsh retorts between them have found their way into our on-line conversations, leaving me in the middle of two friends. Jen recently flew out to San Francisco in what she called a "very different real-life Net-friend experience," where she met up with several other members of our chat room community. Pavel still searches for love on the Internet, and has been involved with several on-line relationships since the Chicago trip.

12. I still hold that it is impossible to fall in love over the Net; there are simply too many variables that cannot be realized until one meets in real life. Friendships abound in the cyberspace community, and after meeting, some on-line friends may form love relationships or even marry, but the high-tech world of atoms is different from the physical world of electrons. Cyberspace relationships can make the crossover and form lifetime bonds, just don't buy those dream house blueprints until after you meet in real life.

B.   Focus on Content

1.   Explain the story to your partner to make sure you understand it. Then put these events into the correct order.

___ Pavel, Jessica, and Jen formed a strong bond.

___ Jessica met Jen in a hotel in Chicago.

___ Jen joined the chat room.

___ Jen and Pavel felt hurt and bitter toward each other all weekend.

___ Jen and Pavel talked for hours every evening.

_1_ Jessica met Pavel in a chat room.

___ Jessica, Jen, and Pavel planned "The Trip."

___ Jen and Pavel met, and hugged tightly.

___ Jen, Pavel, and Jessica still meet sometimes in the chat room.

2.   The author describes Jen and Pavel's relationship as the "classic storybook romance" at the beginning of their relationship. Describe what this means, in your own words, using examples from the story.

_____

_____

_____

3. The author discusses Jen and Pavel's romance throughout the story. Some of her descriptions apply to a traditional romance. Others describe a different kind of relationship that takes place over the Internet. Find two other examples for each category.

Traditional romance	cyberlove
dreamed about a perfect life together	had never physically touched each other
_____	_____
_____	_____

4. The author has a strong point of view about love in cyberspace. Summarize her point of view in two or three sentences.

_____

_____

_____ .

C. Focus on Language

Locate these phrases in the text, using the paragraph number in brackets. Use the context to help you match the phrases that go together.

1. pledged their love (2) _____   a) ridiculed the thought

2. immediate bond (4) _g_   b) plans for a house

3. diversity was the norm (4) _k_   c) speak in a high voice

4. scoffed at the idea (4) _____   d) opinions formed beforehand

5. innermost feelings (5) _____   e) place to meet or gather

6. tight-knit community (5) _____   f) attractive quality

7. squeak out (6) _c_   g) declared their love

8. preconceived notions (9) _____   h) let tensions out

9. alluring characteristic (10) _____   i) private thoughts

10. vent real-life stresses (10) _E_   j) strong connection

11. stomping ground (11) _h_   k) a variety of personalities

12. blueprints (12) _b_   l) close group of friends

Pick-Up Lines

CBC ⊛ LISTENING ACTIVITY 8

A. Prepare to Listen

This listening passage is from "Out Front," a radio show written and produced by teenagers.

First, read these pick-up lines in groups. Then discuss the questions that follow.

Pick-up Lines

Is that love at first sight, or should I walk by again?

Can you see a pay phone? My mom asked me to call when I see the perfect girl.

Can I check the label on your shirt? I want to see if you were made in heaven.

Did it hurt when you fell down from heaven?

I lost my phone number. Can I have yours?

Questions

1. Which of these pick-up lines do you like? Which ones do you dislike?
2. Who uses more pick-up lines, guys or girls?
3. Have you ever used a pick-up line? Did it work?
4. What kind of pick-up lines work best?
5. What is the best pick-up line you ever heard?
6. What is the worst pick-up line you ever heard?
7. What is the funniest pick-up line you ever heard?
8. How would you feel if someone used a pick-up line on you?

B. Listen for Details

Listen and complete the pick-up lines that you hear.

1. You have beautiful _____ .
2. Are you tired? You've been _____ all day.
3. If I were to rearrange the alphabet, I'd put _____ .
4. Was your father a thief? Who stole the _____
    _____ ?
5. King Edward VIII said, "You must miss _____ , eh?"
6. You look _____ , like an absolute intellectual.
7. I'm rich and _____ .

C. Wrap It Up

Listen again. Then discuss these questions with a partner.

1. What personality traits are mentioned in the tape?
2. According to Michael Cunningham, which kinds of pick-up lines generally do not work?
3. What does the woman say about using pick-up lines?
4. What advice does Dr. Cunningham give for meeting women?

Is There a Lid for Every Pot?

A. Prepare to Read

Before you read, scan the article for the expressions below. Then match the expressions with the definitions in the box.

1. live happily ever after (paragraph 1) _____
2. make our dreams come true (paragraph 1) _____
3. were never up to scratch (paragraph 3) _____
4. to stick with (something) (paragraph 4) _____
5. to have second thoughts (paragraph 4) _____
6. to recognize at a glance (paragraph 5) _____
7. come to think of it (paragraph 5) _____
8. to make fun of (someone) (paragraph 6) _____
9. a string of partners (paragraph 9) _____
10. Mr. Right (paragraph 10) _____

---

a) weren't good enough

b) to laugh at (someone)

c) have a successful marriage

d) the ideal man

e) to realize immediately

f) I just remembered

g) fulfil our wishes

h) many different boyfriends/girlfriends

i) to continue with (something)

j) to reconsider

B. Focus on Content

Read the article carefully and answer the questions on pages 111 and 112.

IS THERE A LID FOR EVERY POT?
Melanie Brown

1. Once upon a time, there was a beautiful princess who met a handsome prince and they lived happily ever after. In any case, that's what the fairy tale tells us. Most young people have dreamed that one day they too will meet their one true love and live happily ever after. We have all dreamed that there is one person who is the perfect mate for each of us—the prince or princess who will make our dreams come true.

2. Of course, not all of us are beautiful princesses, nor are we all handsome princes. Yet our culture maintains the myth of the one true love. Popular wisdom tells us that no matter how unattractive or weird a person is, there will be someone, somewhere who is the perfect match. In the words of the old adage, "There's a lid for every pot."

3. The problem, then, is how to find the one true love that destiny has matched us with. If the perfect mate is out there somewhere, shouldn't we just keep searching? All of us know someone who has been involved in the search. My friend Emily wasted most of her adolescence searching vainly for her perfect prince. The guys she dated were never up to scratch. One boyfriend was too tall, another too short, a third too shy, and a fourth had a moustache and was too macho. No one was witty enough or smart enough to be the perfect match for Emily. As soon as she realized her date wasn't the perfect model, he was rejected. "After all, if someone isn't perfect, he can't be my one true love," she used to say.

4. Drummondville psychologist Stephanie Laflamme warns, "People who stick with that childish myth—that there is only one true love for each of us—are unrealistic. When they seek a mate they may well reject a partner who is nearly perfect or at least a pretty good choice. As soon as that person shows a different taste in movies or likes a different pizza topping, it becomes time for second thoughts. The idea that there is only one true love for each of us can create a wrong idea that fate (and not our efforts) will provide us with our perfect partner. 'If that's true, why should we work on building a relationship with someone less than perfect?' we will say.

5. "How many people do you know who are so intelligent, or such big experts in human nature, that they can recognize the perfect mate at a glance?" she asks. Come to think of it, not too many young people (or older ones either) understand themselves so well that they have an infallible list of characteristics to describe the person who can bring them perfect happiness. Someone who seems too quiet or isn't well-educated or isn't good at sports could be rejected. But maybe that same person is playful or funny, and hard working and loyal. And maybe that person loves you and can make you very happy.

6. Experts in love advise a little realism when we select a mate. And don't just look at the surface. Kindness, loyalty and humour may make better long-time traits than cute smiles and being the star of the hockey team in high school. And don't forget that people change. Think of that ugly duckling in high school who grew up to be a swan. Or the nerd you ignored, who is now good-looking and successful. Remember Franco, who Emily made fun of years ago. Now she would do anything to have Franco look at her twice. If Emily had kept her mouth shut then, Franco might have been her Prince Charming today.

7. "In real life, it's not very likely that true love will suddenly smile at us across a crowded room," says school counsellor Jay Martin, "and if it's only the image that attracts you, you are probably heading for trouble." That's not to say that we should give up all our dreams and start thinking that any relationship is better than being alone. Being alone may be far better than marrying a mistake. There is lots of evidence that putting up with anything just to have a relationship doesn't lead to happiness. Plenty of people live alone and have full and happy lives filled with good friends, exciting jobs and sports and hobbies.

8. And rejecting the myth doesn't mean that we should get rid of all our romantic notions either. Life needs poetry and all of us are drawn to different characteristics in other people—there is such a thing as compatibility after all. A person who dislikes opera would probably make a mistake marrying someone whose hobby is playing their favourite CDs of Pavarotti or going to the opera with their mate. A person who wants a big family would probably not find happiness with someone who hates children. And marrying a girl who looks like your mean Aunt Rose probably wouldn't work either.

9. "Many people believe that perfection in a mate is made and not born. But working to develop compatible characteristics in a mate is a more reliable formula than trying out a string of partners looking for the one perfect match" says Stephanie Laflamme.

10. A good marriage is the result of hard work, not a trick of destiny. Even Grandma realized this. She found the best lid she could, and when the lid didn't fit perfectly, she polished it to bring out its best traits. Maybe I should let my friend Emily in on the secret. Her search for Mr. Right isn't going too well lately. She might welcome the advice.

1. "Most people have dreamed that one day they will meet their one true love and live happily ever after," means:
   a) Everyone will probably find a partner one day.
   b) We believe that when we meet our perfect partner, we will be happy for the rest of our lives.
   c) Most people dream about love every night.

2. Our culture maintains the myth that
   a) unattractive and weird people are not very popular.
   b) our dreams are usually about princes and princesses.
   c) somewhere, there is a perfect match for everybody.

3. "There is a lid for every pot" means:
   a) There is a perfect mate for everyone.
   b) It is impossible to find a perfect mate.
   c) No two people are really compatible.

4. The problem with Emily was that
   a) she wasted too much time before she found the perfect guy.
   b) she couldn't find a man good enough for her.
   c) she was looking for a tall man with a moustache.

5. Stephanie Laflamme believes that
   a) love is childish and unrealistic.
   b) fate can lead us to a perfect partner if we search hard enough.
   c) there is more than one person with whom we can have a good relationship.

6. Stephanie Laflamme thinks that
   a) older people probably understand themselves very well.
   b) almost no one can recognize a perfect mate immediately.
   c) it is good to have a list of the characteristics you want.

7. Jay Martin thinks that people get into trouble if
   a) they don't play sports in high school.
   b) they are attracted by superficial characteristics.
   c) they make fun of girls who aren't beautiful or guys who are nerds.

8. The author thinks that
   a) anything is better than someone living alone.
   b) people who live alone can have happy lives.
   c) people who put up with anything are happy.

9. Rejecting the myth of one true love means
   a) being realistic about love.
   b) forgetting about romantic love.
   c) marrying someone who loves opera.

10. Grandma realized that a good marriage comes from
    a) looking for a perfect partner.
    b) working hard at building a successful partnership.
    c) putting up with anything just to have a relationship

C. Focus on Language

Are these words synonyms (the same) or antonyms (opposites)? Write "S" for "synonym," or "A" for "antonym."

1.	myth	reality	_____
2.	weird	normal	_____
3.	adage	saying	_____
4.	destiny	fate	_____
5.	vainly	fruitfully	_____
6.	shy	outgoing	_____
7.	macho	sensitive	_____
8.	seek	search	_____
9.	witty	funny	_____
10.	glance	stare	_____
11.	infallible	unsure	_____
12.	traits	characteristics	_____
13.	evidence	proof	_____
14.	compatibility	friction	_____

Grammar Close-Up

Present Perfect for Indefinite Past Time

Use the **simple past tense** when an action was completed in past time.

EXAMPLE: They **dated** last year.

Use the **present perfect** when the time that an action took place is not known or is not important. Use the **present perfect** for actions that were repeated at an indefinite time in the past.

EXAMPLES: Julie **has dated** Robert for a long time.
             I **have talked** to him many times on the phone.

Use the present form (**has, have**) of the auxiliary verb. Use the past participle of the main verb.

For many verbs, the past tense and the past participle are the same.

EXAMPLE: I **walked**. I **have walked**.

Other verbs use an irregular form for the past participle.

EXAMPLE: I **ate**. I **have eaten**.

Some common irregular forms of the past participle are listed below. For a complete list see Appendix 2 on page 175.

Base form	Past tense	Past participle
become	became	become
begin	began	begun
come	came	come
drink	drank	drunk
eat	ate	eaten
drive	drove	driven
give	gave	given
go	went	gone
know	knew	known
run	ran	run
see	saw	seen
speak	spoke	spoken
take	took	taken
wear	wore	worn
write	wrote	written

A.   Choose the correct verb and put it in the present perfect form.

meet   introduce   see   write   cook   give   chat   take   travel   flirt

1. John and Jenny _____ that movie together several times.

2. Lise _____ with Donald on the Internet a few times.

3. Janet _____ some long letters to her boyfriend.

4. Henri _____ some great pictures of his new girlfriend.

5. My sister _____ books of love poems to her fiancé.

6. Tanya and Mike _____ to Europe together several times.

7. Marc _____ some special dinners for Melanie.

8. Tara _____ Jeff for coffee many times.

9. Alice _____ people to each other quite a few times.

10. My brother _____ with many girls in the last year.

B. Choose the **simple past** or the **present perfect** form of the verb.

1. Jen and Pavel (hugged / have hugged) when they met.

2. Emily (dated / has dated) some weirdos lately.

3. Emily (dated / has dated) a very good-looking guy last Saturday.

4. Philip and Anne (took / have taken) some great pictures with their new camera.

5. Jack proposed when he (realized / has realized) he loved Kate.

6. Paul (knew / has known) right away that Karine was the right girl for him.

7. Luc (thought / has thought) that Annie was very attractive.

8. Luc (thought / has thought) about Annie many times.

9. Jim and Lily (fell in love / have fallen in love) last year.

10. My mother (told / has told) me frequently that I am too fussy.

C. Complete the sentences using the **simple past** or the **present perfect**.

1. Tara _____ (ask) Ben out on a date.

2. Jack _____ (ask) questions about the new girl in his class many times.

3. My parents _____ (meet) when they were in their early 20s.

4. My grandparents _____ (return) to Niagara Falls frequently.

5. Catherine _____ (invite) her boyfriend's parents for dinner last Sunday.

6. There is a rumour that Andy and Barbara _____ (fall) in love.

7. Mike and Sue _____ (go) out for a romantic dinner last night.

8. My sister _____ (love) Sam since high school.

9. That couple _____ (be) together for many years.

10. Suddenly true love _____ (smile) at us across the room.

Negative

The **negative** of the **present perfect** refers to actions or events that have not happened at the time you are speaking.

EXAMPLE: He **has dated** many girls, but he **hasn't fallen** in love.

Use **never** with the **present perfect** to refer to an action that has not happened at any time.

EXAMPLE: She **has never dated** anyone she works with. (not at any time)

!

Do not use **never** with a negative verb. Double negatives are not used in English.

> I **have never asked** a guy out. ✔
>
> I haven't never asked a guy out. ✗

A.   Choose the correct verb to complete the sentences. Use the negative form of the **present perfect**. Use contractions.

meet   spend   accepted   speak   miss   go   plan   do   fall   introduce

1. Those guys _____ to us yet.

2. She _____ anything to cause problems in her relationships.

3. My friend _____ me to that cute guy yet.

4. Tina _____ anyone on the Internet so far.

5. Bill and Lori _____ their wedding yet.

6. I _____ to a great party for a long time.

7. We _____ much money on long distance calls.

8. Jen and Pavel _____ a day without chatting on the Internet.

9. Maxine _____in love yet.

10. My family _____ my new romance.

Question Form

Use the **present perfect** for questions when you don't want to focus on when an action occurred. Use the **simple past** when the time an action occurred is mentioned. Look at the examples.

EXAMPLES: **Have you ever fallen** in love? (at any time in your life)

> **Did** you **fall** in love last summer?

Ever ("at any time") is often used with questions about indefinite past time. **Ever** follows the auxiliary verb and subject, and goes before the main verb.

EXAMPLE: Have you **ever** gone on a blind date?

On the chart, check the activities you **have done**. Then interview three other students to see if they **have ever done** these things. Write the names of the students you interview. Ask the question "Have you ever ...?"

Name	Me			
fallen in love				
gone on a blind date				
dated someone much older than you				
cooked dinner for someone you love				
gone out with two people at once				
cried over someone you love				
used a pick-up line				
told someone you love him or her				
had a summer romance				
fallen in love on the Internet				
behaved badly in a relationship				
done something foolish for love				
sent flowers to someone you love				
written a love poem				
dated someone with blond hair				
thought about your wedding				
eaten pizza on a date				
dreamed about your perfect love				
held hands on a first date				
dated a friend of your brother or sister				

Two Sides to Every Question

Choose one of the following subjects. When the teacher calls your name, talk for one or two minutes to support **Statement A**. When the teacher says "Stop," switch to **Statement B**, and give arguments to support it. The class will decide which of your arguments is most convincing.

1. **Statement A:** Love is controlled by destiny.
   Statement B: You have to work hard to have a great relationship.

2. **Statement A:** It's possible to fall in love at first sight.
   Statement B: You can't fall in love at first sight.

3. **Statement A:** It's better to be alone and happy than to be in a bad relationship.
   Statement B: It's better to be with someone than to be alone.

4. **Statement A:** Girls are more romantic than guys.
   Statement B: Guys are more romantic than girls.

5. **Statement A:** People who have the same interests usually end up together.
   Statement B: Opposites attract.

6. **Statement A:** Girls and guys can be just friends.
   Statement B: It's impossible for girls and guys to be just friends.

Write About It

Focus on Supporting Details

Write a four-paragraph composition about the qualities that are most important to you in a relationship. First make an outline listing your topic sentences and supporting details. Support can be provided with examples, details, statistics, descriptions, or reasons. Then develop each paragraph, using support. Each paragraph should have at least three pieces of support.

Where to Find Friends

Don't Take Them Out With You!

Some expressions may sound grammatically correct in English, but are, in fact, typical Gallicisms!

A.   Look at the words or expressions in bold. Then check the list below to see if you can find the words that are really your friends in English.

1.   We **passed** the weekend skiing at Mont Ste. Anne.

2.   I teach English, but my **formation** is in graphic design.

3.   St. Catherine Street is not very **large**.

4.   Someone **closed** the television while I was out of the room.

5.   I have a **reunion** with my group tomorrow.

6.   Jean-Pierre had a skiing accident but luckily he is **correct**.

7.   Suzanne was **deceived** with her marks on the mid-term exams.

8.   I can't see anything. Could someone please **open** the lights.

9.   The **animator** of the game show is really popular with the viewers.

10. Frederique has been doing some **experiences** in the physics lab.

11. At my house we always **recuperate** newspapers.

12. People were angry about the new law, and there were **manifestations**.

13. I love basketball. I'm really **sportif**.

14. There are a lot of **publicities** about the new hemp products.

turned off   host   demonstrations   disappointed   spent   experiments
turn on   athletic   wide   background/training   advertisements   all right
meeting   recycle

B.   Write out the sentences with the words you should use in English.

This Unit Is X-Rated

Learning Objectives

In this unit you will:

- listen to an interview with the man who invented the digital signs in the Montreal subway

- practise expressing agreement and disagreement

- read about teenagers' use of swear words

- watch a video about swearing in advertising

- learn about the present perfect and present perfect continuous for duration of time

YOUR DAILY SMILE:

As empty vessels make the loudest sound, so they that have the least wit are the greatest babblers.

—*Plato*

billboerd ; l'anneau publicitaire

Non-Stop Talking

In groups of three or four, talk about these questions. Keep talking for 20 minutes. Be prepared to give the class a summary of your group's ideas and information.

1. List some kinds of advertising you see on a daily basis.

2. When commercials come on between TV shows, do you watch them? Why or why not?

3. What kinds of TV commercials appeal to you? Explain why.

4. What kinds of TV commercials do you dislike? Explain why.

5. What was the best TV commercial you ever saw? Describe it.

6. What was the worst TV commercial you ever saw? Describe it.

7. What kinds of magazine or newspaper ads capture your interest?

8. What kinds of gimmicks are used in ads to attract attention?

9. Describe the funniest or most unusual ad you have ever seen.

10. What kinds of ads do you notice outside?

11. How effective are these ads in influencing you to buy things?

12. What kinds of things are advertised in public places such as subways or shopping malls?

13. Do you find ads in subways or buses to be helpful and informative? Why or why not?

14. Were you ever upset or angry about an ad you saw? Explain what offended you.

15. Did you ever hear swearing on a TV ad? What was the ad for?

16. Do TV ads reflect the way people really act and talk? Explain your answer.

17. How do you feel if you hear people swearing in public?

18. How would you feel about hearing swearing in TV ads?

19. Are there any situations where you would not like to hear swearing?

20. Do you think using swear words can be effective in selling things?

Messenger of the Metro
LISTENING ACTIVITY 9
Interview with an Advertising Specialist

A.   Read the following paragraph quickly. Then close your book and write as the teacher dictates.

Have you been in the Montreal metro lately? Something funny is going on. It's the visual display boards that give corresponding bus and train information. They also offer riders news and sports reports, television listings, lottery numbers, and animated advertisements. Some people call them "free entertainment."

Did you know that Montreal is the first city to have these display boards? Did you know that the concept and technology was developed by a Montrealer, Mr. Marshall Moreyne?

B.   First, read the questions with a partner. Then listen to the interview and answer the questions.

1.   What idea occurred to Marshall when he saw the electronic display module in a store?

2.   What percentage of people have a positive reaction to the advertisements in the Montreal metro?

3.   How does Marshall know that people like the ads?

4.   How effective are the ads, compared with television?

5.   Name some products and services that are sold through the metro ads.

6.   Why are the metro ads such an effective medium?

7.   Give two ways the ads are targeted to students.

8.   Which other cities will soon have the animated ads?

9.   Explain how the animators convert the storyboards into ads.

South Park

A. Focus on Vocabulary

Read this paragraph. Put in the words to complete the sentences.

complaints   coarse   aired   loyal   reflection   crudely   offensive   defend

South Park is a television show that has a **1** _loyal_ following among teenagers. The show features **2** _crudely_ drawn cartoons and **3** _coarse_ language that is **4** _offensive_ to some people. For this reason, the show is now **5** _complete_ late in the evening. The show's producers have received some **6**_____ about the coarse language, but they **7**_____ their program by saying it captures the way people really speak. They say their show is a **8**_____ of reality.

B. Focus on Language

Discuss the questions below, using these expressions to show agreement or disagreement when needed.

I believe…   I agree with…/I don't agree with…
I think…   According to…(someone)
In my opinion…   From my point of view…

!

It's incorrect to say "I'm agree with that/I'm not agree with that."

It's incorrect to say "according to me…" although it's correct to say "According to (name of another person)…"

1. What does "PG" mean?

2. What kinds of shows are rated "PG"?

3. Do you think parents should censor what their children see or hear? If so, what kinds of things should they censor?

4. At what age should children be allowed to choose what they watch or listen to?

5. Should children's language be censored (for example, not allowing them to use swear words)? Why or why not?

6. Who uses swear words the most?

7. Are there negative consequences of using swear words?

8. Have you watched the show *South Park*? Explain why you like or dislike the show.

9. Do you think *South Park* is offensive? Why or why not?

10. Do you think children should be allowed to watch shows like *South Park*? Why or why not?

This Story Is Rated PG

A. Focus on Expressions

These are some phrases or expressions from the story. Check (✔) the ones that refer to swearing.

✔ curse	✔ scraps of conversation
✔ use coarse language	___ catch sight of
✔ adapting language	___ foul-mouthed *mauvaise bouche.*
___ animated conversation	✔ profanity addiction
___ slang	✔ crude language
✔ mouth like a sewer	___ being malicious
___ use caution	✔ language discrimination
✔ feel deviant	✔ offensive language
___ emulate language	___ being naive
✔ string of obscenities	___ mouth off *parler d'une manière vulgaire*

B. Focus on Opinions

Discuss these sentences in groups. Write "A" for "Agree" or "D" for "Disagree" in the column under "Your opinion."

	Your opinion	Author's opinion
1. The average teenager swears more than the characters on *South Park*.		
2. Many teenagers don't even realize they are swearing.	A	
3. In general, boys swear more than girls.		D
4. Teenagers today generally swear in private, rather than in public.		
5. Teenagers swear more when they are together in groups.		

6. Swearing amongst teenagers seems to be declining.   _____   _____

7. Most students know when to swear and when not to.   _____   _____

8. Movies and television talk shows probably contribute to the kinds of language students use.   _____   _____

9. Adults feel the same way about swearing as teenagers do.   _____   _____

10. Swearing isn't high on the list of concerns for most teenagers.   _____   _____

C. Focus on General Ideas

Read the story quickly and decide if the author agrees or disagrees with each sentence. Write "A" for "Agree" or "D" for "Disagree" in the column under "Author's opinion." Compare the two columns. How many of your opinions were the same as the author's?

This Story Is Rated PG

Basem Boshra

Warning: This story contains coarse language and, due to its content, should not be read by anyone!

1. If you thought the animated characters on the wildly popular *South Park* cartoon were foul-mouthed, you should start listening more closely to Montreal teenagers. You've probably passed them countless times this summer: packs of teens hanging out in shopping malls, in front of movie theatres or in fast-food restaurants. Chances are their conversations were peppered with some or all of the words you can't say on television.

2. For many teens, those words seem to have replaced nouns, verbs, and adjectives in their speech. "It's pretty common," said Eric Lemay, 15. "I think it's become more like slang than something offensive. Even my parents talk like that with me. I think a lot of us do it without thinking about it. You hear everybody else doing it and you start swearing without realizing it."

3. Boys like Jesse Larson, a 15-year-old student hanging out at a video arcade, admitted to having a mouth like a sewer. "All the time," replied Larson when asked how often he swore. "With my friends, at home, at school, everywhere. I can't control it." Larson wasn't exaggerating. Just minutes before admitting to his pro-fanity addiction, he hurled a string of obscenities at the arcade machine that had just informed him his game was over.

4. English, French, boys, girls—there's little discrimination when it comes to cursing. "Definitely," said 16-year-old Jenna McNiece when asked whether she swore as much as the boys she knows. "And if I'm in a bad mood, I probably do it a lot more."

5. What interests psychologist Donald Taylor about teen swearing is not the fact that it happens, but where. "Let's not be naïve," said Taylor. "Teenagers have always cursed, but when did they do it? They would do it in private, in hockey locker

rooms, for example. But occasionally it would slip out in public, and people would be a bit shocked and the teenagers would feel somewhat deviant."

6.   Today, Taylor said, teens swear when they're out together to show that they belong to a group. "It becomes a mark of group identity. For a group to have an identity, it must be different, or else it's not distinguishable from others. So developing a distinct "language" is essential. And that's where the swearing comes in."

7.   Robert Morrison, a high-school principal, said swearing among his students is on the rise. "We definitely have to caution the kids in the halls about it more than we used to." But Morrison said the vast majority of students know better than to mouth off to their teachers, which results in immediate suspension. He hands down about one such suspension a month. "Even in those situations, it's normally someone who's frustrated or angry about something. Nothing malicious."

8.   In fact, Morrison said, most students are quite wary about their language around him and their teachers. "They'll catch sight of one of us as we're walking by and say, 'Oh sorry sir, it just slipped out.'" Fifteen-year-old Luke Edwards said, "You have to pick your spots. I don't swear at my parents or at teachers because that's a stupid thing to do."

9.   Movies, television and music can play a big role in shaping teens' colourful language, said sociologist Lyle Robinson. "When you watch a Quentin Tarantino or Coen brothers film, you see they've taken swearing to a whole new level. They've transformed it into a kind of hip vernacular, something that, far from being deviant, is to be emulated.

10.   The same names pop up over and over when teens talk about their favourite entertainment: crude cartoons like *South Park* and *Beavis and Butthead*, trash-talk shows like Jenny Jones, and raunchy radio DJ Howard Stern.

11.   Yet many teens refuse to believe that pop culture affects the way they talk. "I watch those shows because they're funny," said Brian Stewart, 17, "but I don't swear because I watch them. That's ridiculous."

12.   Donald Taylor doesn't think it's ridiculous. He said the repeated exposure to coarse language of such shows has to have some effect on teens. "It's the same arguments that people have made about violence on television," Taylor said. "A lot of the evidence shows that it doesn't directly make you more violent, but it de-sensitizes you to it. Your threshold, or what you perceive as normal, increases."

13.   Swear words still haven't lost their ability to shock some people. Abigail Morris, 67, hears teenagers talking on the bus, and says, "It's just awful some of the things they say. If I had said some of those words as a child, I would have gotten a good punishment."

14.   But it seems that for most teens, swearing isn't high on their list of concerns. "To tell you the truth, until you asked me about it I can honestly say I've never thought about it," said 17-year old Marshall Grant. "If we swear too much or too little, who cares?" They're just words.

D.   Focus on Language

Highlight these expressions in the text. Then circle the letter of the words or phrases with a similar meaning. Use the context to help you.

1.   countless times (paragraph 1)
     a) not many times
     b) very often

2. were peppered with (paragraph 1)
   a) used frequently
   b) used rarely

3. It would slip out. (paragraph 5)
   a) They would say things without realizing it.
   b) They would say things to get people's attention.

4. feel deviant (paragraph 5)
   a) feel smarter than the others
   b) feel as if they were doing something wrong

5. mouth off (paragraph 7)
   a) say what's on their minds
   b) speak inappropriately

6. wary (about their language) (paragraph 8)
   a) careful
   b) unconscious

7. You have to pick your spots. (paragraph 8)
   a) You must express yourself clearly.
   b) You have to choose your moment.

8. hip vernacular (paragraph 9)
   a) new, modern way to speak
   b) rude way to express yourself

9. It de-sensitizes you. (paragraph 12)
   a) makes it easier for you to accept something
   b) makes you too sensitive to accept something

10. their list of concerns (paragraph 14)
    a) things they worry about
    b) things they don't understand

The F-Word

CBC VIDEO ACTIVITY 6

A.   Read the questions with a partner. As you watch the video, answer the questions. Write only the **key words**. Don't try to write full sentences.

1. Which of these words are given in the dictionary definition of the word "swear"?

   ✓ profane   ✓ naughty   ✓ obnoxious *détestable*
   ___ profound   ✓ taboo   ___ high-class
   ✓ funny   ✓ outrageous   ✓ anti-social
   ✓ dirty   ✓ low-class   ___ silly

2. Name two places where you often hear swearing.

   _____ *class , radio* _____

3. What does Timothy Jay, the New York professor, identify as the "good aspect" of swearing?

   _____ *express deep emotion* _____

4. Why do many Toronto teenagers listen to "Humble and Fred"?

   _____

5. Who works on the telecaster committee?

   _____ *Censors* _____

6. How does Pat Beatty explain why certain words are unacceptable?

   _____ *other family* _____

7. How does Professor Jay explain the absence of swear words in TV ads?

   _____ *Wanted of aspects* _____

8. Ad companies want to "get hip, get real...and get attention," but there is a fine line between _____ *most* _____ people _____ *turning* _____ and _____ people _____ *insult.* _____.

9. What kind of people are chosen for "focus groups"?

   _____ *Carfully Canadian* _____

10. What does the ad man say about the word "flabgorst"?

    _____ *it his is funny* _____

11. What do advertisers want to find out from Professor Jay?

    _____

12. What point did Donna McCarthy want to make in her ad for the food bank?

    _____ *To sell a card* _____

13. How did the focus group's attitude change after they saw Donna's ad for the food bank?

    _____ *that the t* _____

14. What two things happened with Donna's ad for the food bank?

    _____ *trade aroredo* _____

B. Write a summary of the video.

Grammar Close-Up

Present Perfect and Present Perfect Continuous for Duration of Time

Present Perfect

Use the **present perfect** to suggest duration of time. Use it to focus on an action or state that started in the past and continues in the present.

Use the auxiliary verb **have (has)** with the past participle of the main verb. See a list of irregular past participles in Appendix 2 on page 175.

EXAMPLES: She **has worked** there for two years. (And she still does.)

We **have known** each other since we were kids. (And we still do.)

A.   Look at the chart of verbs that are used to express duration of time in the present perfect. Then complete the sentences with the present perfect form of one of the verbs on the list.

Base form	Past tense	Past participle
be	was, were	been
go	went	gone (to school)
have	had	had
know	knew	known
live	lived	lived
speak	spoke	spoken (a language)
work	worked	worked

1. Mike and Frannie _____ neighbours for six years.

2. Carla _____ Italian since she was a child.

3. Sam and Max _____ at the supermarket for ages.

4. Tina and I _____ to the same college for the past year.

5. My mother _____ the head librarian for many years.

6. Carrie _____ in my neighbourhood since we were kids.

7. Jim _____ this car for at least three years.

8. Paul _____ for an engineering company since June.

9. Lise _____ Stan since elementary school.

10. We _____ in residence since we started college.

Present Perfect Questions Related to Duration of Time

When questions use the **present perfect** to refer to duration of time, the expression **long** or **how long** is often used.

EXAMPLES: Have you been here **long**? No, just ten minutes.

How long have you lived in Punta Arenas? (for) five years

A.   Read the sentences. Write questions to help you get more information. Use **how long** and the **present perfect**.

EXAMPLE: Denis is a student. **How long has Denis been a student?**

1. Denis lives in Toronto.

2. He goes to a technical college.

3. Denis's relatives have a store.

4. Denis works in the store on weekends.

5. He knows a girl from Montreal.

6. They are in the same classes.

7. She speaks French.

8. Her family lives in Montreal.

9. She works in the school library.

10. They are good friends.

Present Perfect Continuous

The **present perfect continuous** describes an action that began in the past, is progressive and is still continuing in the present. Use **have/has + been +** present participle of the main verb.

EXAMPLES: The guy next door **has been playing** the tuba all afternoon.

I **have been waiting** for you for more than an hour.

A.   Choose the correct verb and complete the sentences using the present perfect continuous form of the verb.

wait   study   swear   use   sleep   try   watch   shock   play   drive

1. Where were you? I _____ to reach you all day.

2. Teenagers _____ their parents for generations.

3. Those boys _____ since the teacher left the room.

4. We're tired because we _____ for the exam all night.

5. Marco is so lazy. He _____ all day long.

6. That ad is famous because jeans companies _____ it everywhere.

7. Joey used to swear a lot, but lately he _____ his language.

8. I'm angry at Ally. I _____ here for her since three o'clock.

9. The same film _____ at this theatre for nearly a month.

10. Suzy needs a rest. She _____ on the highway for hours.

B.   Put the sentences below into the question form. Then answer them in the negative using the present continuous form.

EXAMPLE: Valerie has been getting enough sleep lately.

Has Valerie been getting enough sleep lately?

Valerie hasn't been getting enough sleep lately.

1. Paul has been spending time on the Internet recently.

2. That guy has been using rough language in class.

3. Those students have been watching South Park on TV.

4. The teachers have been noticing an increase in swearing lately.

5. Teenagers have been copying the language their friends use.

6. TV has been transforming swearing into a hip new vernacular.

7. The language teens use in the bus has been shocking people.

8. Teens have been using more vulgar language than in the past.

9. Parents have been complaining about the language kids use.

10.   Sally has been checking the Internet for information on movie stars.

Two Sides to Every Question

Choose one of the following subjects. When the teacher calls your name, talk for one or two minutes to support **Statement A**. When the teacher says "Stop," switch to **Statement B**, and give arguments to support it. The class will decide which of your arguments is most convincing.

1. **Statement A:** Swearing is pretty much accepted in society today. Everyone swears sometimes, and most people know when to watch their language.

    Statement B: Swearing is bad language. No one should use it.

2. **Statement A:** Teenagers today swear too much.

    Statement B: Swearing is no big deal. Everyone does it.

3. **Statement A:** TV shows shouldn't use swear words.

    Statement B: TV shows should reflect reality.

4. **Statement A:** Movies and TV shows should have ratings to tell people how much swearing or violence they contain.

    Statement B: People can judge for themselves if they want to watch a movie or TV show. Ratings reflect just one opinion about what's appropriate.

UNIT 10

Take Care of Yourself

Learning Objectives

In this unit you will:

- discuss health and natural remedies

- read about herbal remedies

- review reflexive pronouns

- listen to an interview about workplace massage

- write a composition about health

- learn about the passive voice

YOUR DAILY SMILE
It takes 43 muscles to frown, but only 17 to smile—so if you want to save energy, smile!

Non-Stop Talking

In groups of three or four, talk about these questions. Keep talking for 20 minutes. Be prepared give the class a summary of your group's ideas and information.

1. How important is your health to you?
2. Do you do anything in particular to stay healthy?
3. What kinds of foods are important for good health?
4. What other kinds of activities contribute to good health?
5. What are some of the things students do that are bad for their health?
6. How often do you get minor illnesses such as colds?
7. What do you do if you get a cold?
8. What are some sources of stress in society today?
9. What are the biggest sources of stress for students?
10. What kinds of illnesses are related to stress?
11. What can you do if you are feeling a lot of stress?
12. How often do you go to a doctor for a check-up?
13. How do you decide if you should see a doctor when you're not feeling well?
14. Do you ever use "natural" or herbal remedies for health problems? Explain what you use.
15. How are new medications tested?
16. Should new medications be tested on people?
17. Would you participate in testing new drugs to help medical science?
18. Are there any dangers for volunteers who test new medications?
19. What are some of the health problems students have today that were not a problem a generation ago?
20. How can students protect themselves from these problems?

Pronunciation Close-Up

Work in pairs. Say the words below. Then mark the primary stress in each word.

remedies   herbalism   indigestion   beverages   modern   physician
respiratory   ingredient   stomach   congestion   percentage   irresponsible
scientists   develop

Healing Herbs

A.   What do you know about herbal remedies? Work in pairs. Find the best answer for each question.

1. Which of these is an herb?
    a) coffee   c) ginger
    b) tea   d) all of the above

2. Tea can be used to:
    a) clean your breath   c) prevent asthma attacks
    b) help prevent tooth decay

3. An ancient Chinese drink that evolved into something we use today for indigestion is:
    a) coffee   c) club soda
    b) ginger ale

4. Coca-cola began as an attempt to cure:
    a) cold sores   c) headaches
    b) insomnia

5. People munch on this to freshen their breath after a meal:
    a) lemon   c) parsley
    b) celery

6. Which headache remedy was created from two healing herbs?
    a) Tylenol   c) Aspirin
    b) Anacin

7. Which herb is effective in treating tooth decay?
    a) ginger   c) peppermint
    b) garlic

8. Which flavour used in cough medicine comes from an herb?
    a) blueberry   c) grape
    b) cherry

9. Which of these is recommended for motion sickness?
    a) garlic   c) aloe
    b) ginger

10. Which of these is recommended for a healthy heart?
    a) garlic   c) cucumber
    b) peanuts

B.   Skim the article to check your answers.

A. Coffee, Coke, and Clorets

When was the last time you used a healing herb? You may not realize it, but you use herbs that have medicinal properties all the time. We all do. Perhaps you started your day with a

HEALING HERBS
Michael Castleman

cup of coffee or tea. Coffee is not only America's favourite morning stimulant, but scientists have shown it's also an effective bronchial decongestant. Tea is less stimulating than coffee, but it has also been found to be an effective decongestant. And it's a good source of fluoride, so it would help in preventing tooth decay.

Do you enjoy soft drinks? Most of today's carbonated beverages were originally herbal medicines. Thousands of years ago, the ancient Chinese drank ginger tea for indigestion, a use supported by modern science. During Elizabethan times, the English developed their own ginger-based stomach soother, ginger beer, which evolved into today's ginger ale.

Coca-Cola began as an attempt to develop an herbal headache remedy. Coke was invented in the 1880s by an Atlanta pharmacist who stocked the tropical kola nut because 19th century physicians prescribed it to treat respiratory ailments. Not too long ago, an article in the *Journal of the American Medical Association* suggested giving cola drinks to children with asthma as preventive medication.

The last time you dined out, did your plate come with a sprig of pars-ley? Parsley garnishes are another echo of herbal healing. People used to munch this herb to freshen their breath after meals. Parsley is high in the breath-sweetening plant pigment chlorophyll—the Clor in Clorets breath mints and one of the active ingredients in Certs.

And speaking of restaurants, perhaps your last check arrived with an after-dinner mint. These candies harken back to ancient times, when people sipped mint tea after feasts to settle their stomachs, another traditional medicinal use supported by modern science.

B. The Source of Today's Drugs

America's medicine cabinets are filled with drugs. Did you know the very word "drug" links us to herbal healing? It comes from the early German *droge*, meaning "to dry," as in drying herbs, the first step in processing herbs into medicines. But the link goes beyond word origins. Many drugs in home medicine cabinets have herbal roots.

Aspirin was originally created from two healing herbs, white willow bark and meadowsweet. In fact, meadowsweet's old scientific name, Spirea, gives us the spirin in aspirin.

For the congestion of colds, flu, or hay fever, millions of Americans reach for Sudafed. Its active ingredient, pseudoephedrine, was developed from the world's oldest healing herb, ma huang, which Chinese physicians have prescribed for 5,000 years to treat chest congestion.

Thousands of years ago, people noticed that several aromatic herbs helped treat tooth pain. We now know tooth decay and gum disease are caused by oral bacteria, and science has shown that the herbs traditionally used to treat dental ailments kill these germs. One antibacterial herb is peppermint, which is why peppermint oil (menthol) is an ingredient in many toothpastes. An active component of thyme—thymol—is an ingredient in Listerine.

If there are children in your home, chances are there's a cherry-flavoured cough syrup in your medicine cabinet. The cherry flavour is no accident. The American Indians treated coughs with wild cherry bark, and we're still using it today.

C. A Blind Spot in Medical Training

British and European physicians often prescribe herbal medicines along with—or instead of—pharmaceuticals. Some American physicians support herbal healing, but most remain sceptical. Some are downright hostile. Why?

The answer has to do with a major blind spot in American medical training. Medical schools ignore the history of healing, so most physicians have no idea that until this century, most medicines were herbal. And pharmacology professors rarely mention that a large percentage of U.S. prescription medications are still derived from plants.

From time to time, a leading medical journal reports an herb's effectiveness. For example, a recent report in the Journal of the National Cancer Institute suggests that garlic prevents stomach cancer. But most herb studies are published in obscure journals (many in German), publications the typical physician never sees. As a result, most American doctors are unfamiliar with the vast scientific literature demonstrating herbs' safety and effectiveness for an enormous number of ills.

The sad fact is, the typical American physician's only real exposure to herbal healing involves the small but steady stream of medical journal articles reporting harm from the irresponsible use of healing herbs. The number of people harmed by herbs is only a tiny fraction of the number harmed by pharmaceuticals and accepted medical procedures. Nonetheless, most of what physicians know about herbs is decidedly negative, so it's no wonder they feel sceptical of herbal healing.

Fortunately, this situation is changing as herb studies make their way into more prestigious journals. Headache specialists now recommend feverfew to prevent migraines because several well-publicized studies have shown its effectiveness. Many physicians now suggest ginger to prevent motion sickness and the nausea associated with cancer chemotherapy because a study published in the respected British medical journal *Lancet* shows that it prevents nausea better than a standard treatment, Dramamine. Many cardiologists now recommend a diet high in garlic, based on studies showing it to be remarkably effective in reducing cholesterol and other risk factors for heart disease.

Scientists are taking a new look at a whole gamut of ancient healing remedies. And in the process, they are taking the guesswork and the hocus-pocus out of using nature's medicines. It is now easier—and safer—than ever to take advantage of the healing power of herbs.

C. Read parts B and C of the article and answer the questions.

1. What does the word "drug" mean?

    _____

2. Which physicians often use herbal medicines today? Which physicians are often sceptical?

    _____

3. What is the "blind spot" in American medical training?

    _____

4. Why do American doctors know so little about herbs?

    _____

5. What information do most American doctors receive about herbs?

    _____

6. How does the number of people harmed by herbs compare with the number harmed by pharmaceuticals?

    _____

Grammar Close-Up

Reflexive Pronouns

Use a **reflexive pronoun** when the subject and object of a sentence are the same person.

EXAMPLE: Steve taught **himself** English.

Use a reflexive pronoun with **by** to mean **alone**.

EXAMPLES: Suzanne went to the party **by herself**.

            We went to the exercise class **by ourselves**.

Reflexive pronouns have the singular ending **self** or the plural ending **selves**.

myself	ourselves
yourself	yourselves
himself	themselves
herself	
itself	

!

Activities that are normally done alone, such as washing, shaving, or combing your hair, are not used with reflexive pronouns in English.

EXAMPLE: ✘ He shaved himself.   ✔ He shaved.

A.   Use reflexive pronouns to complete the sentences.

1. Tina doesn't get sick often because she knows how to take care of _____.

2. Some people can cure _____ of minor illnesses.

3. If you are really sick you should go to the doctor rather than try to cure _____.

4. You and Jean can serve _____ some ginger ale.

5. My brother protects _____ from injury by stretching before he exercises.

6. People with colds can help _____ get better by resting in bed.

7. We used the scale at the gym to weigh _____.

8. Diana introduced _____ when she came into the room.

9. The black cat got up and scratched _____.

10. I wasn't feeling well so I excused _____ and went home.

B.   Complete the sentences. Use **by** + a reflexive pronoun to replace the word **alone**.

EXAMPLE: Curing high blood pressure is hard to do alone.   **by yourself**

1. Thank you, but I can open this medicine bottle alone. _____

2. You can't treat a heart attack alone. _____

3. Swimming is an activity that people often do alone. _____

4. Did you go to the hospital alone? _____

5. I found the doctor's office alone. _____

6. Did Lisa cure her infection alone? _____

7. We answered the questionnaire alone. _____

8. The nurse treated that sick patient alone. _____

9. My father treated his minor burn alone. _____

10. Those scientists found cures for some diseases alone. _____

Workplace Massage

 LISTENING ACTIVITY 10

Stress is very common these days. This listening passage is about a new way to reduce stress on the job: workplace massage.

First, read the questions with a partner. Then, as you listen, answer the questions. Write **key words** only.

1. Circle two reasons that are given for stress in the workplace.

   cutbacks   pay cuts   downsizing   messy work

2. Name two characteristics of the type of workplace that offers massage to employees. _____

3. Which two body parts does a massage therapist often work on in an office? _____

4. What happens in the special massage room?

   _____

5. Name three activities that cause workplace tension.

   _____

6. Name two reactions that people can have when they release tension after a massage. _____

7. Massage affects babies by increasing _____
   and _____ .

8. According to Dr. Tiffany Fields, what are three benefits of massage?

   a) _____

   b) _____

   c) _____

9. When did massage first begin? _____

10. What did Hippocrates say about medicine in 400 B.C.?

    _____

11. What did Ira say about the idea of bringing massage to the radio station?

    yes   no   maybe

12. What happens at the end of the interview?

    _____

The Guinea Pig

Read the following paragraph quickly. Then close your book and write as the teacher dictates.

A guinea pig is a small furry rodent. It makes a good pet because it seldom bites and is easy to care for. The guinea pig is best known for its contribution to science, however. Guinea pigs are often used in research, to develop new drugs, and to test fields of behaviour, nutrition, and heredity. When people are used in tests, they are often called "human guinea pigs."

Sell Yourself to Science

A. Prepare to Read

Read the ad below. Would you answer this ad?

MediLab International

MediLab International is a research company conducting studies on a wide range of medications. Its modern research centre is currently recruiting participants for a study:

Non-smoking men or women, between 18 and 35 years of age, available to stay at our clinic from Monday night to Wednesday afternoon.

$300.00

If you are interested in participating or would like further information, please contact us today.

B. Focus on Topic Sentences

1. Skim the article on page 140 to find out what it's about. Then write the number of the paragraph that corresponds to each phrase below. Paragraph 1 is the introduction. Omit that paragraph.

    ____ some problems or dangers of volunteering

    ____ the reason volunteers are needed

    ____ which people generally volunteer to test drugs

    ____ less invasive treatments to be tested

    ____ the reasons students volunteer

2. Which sentence in each paragraph tells you what the paragraph is about? Find the topic sentence in each paragraph and use a highlighter to identify it.

Sell Yourself to Science

Laura Petrecca

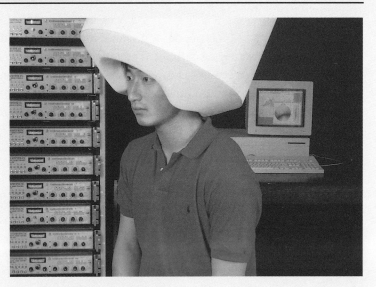

1.   Over two weekends, Albert, a university student, earned $400 while watching large-screen TV, playing pool, and viewing the latest videos. Has he found the perfect internship? No: he earned his pay by becoming a human guinea pig. Albert tested drug absorption rates at a Baltimore company that pays test participants $100 a day. Albert was paid to take a drug designed to lower blood pressure. He then spent his weekend sitting around while staff members took blood samples to test how well the medication had been absorbed.

2.   Volunteers such as Albert are needed for clinical research because government agencies won't approve any new or altered medication that has not been tested on humans. These drugs are first studied through lab and animal testing, and if approved, tried on healthy volunteers to determine safety and dosage. Before final approval, a drug must be tested by volunteers who have the disease or condition, to determine factors such as effectiveness and adverse reactions.

3.   In many of the thousands of research sites, 25% to 35% of volunteers are college students. "Students are amongst the best markets because they don't have full-time jobs and can find the time for testing," says one of the researchers. Researchers say that those who are unemployed or lacking medical insurance, retirees, and seasonal and part-time workers also volunteer.

4.   Money is the main motivator for student participants. Other factors include free treatment or an interest in medical science. And although this testing may not bring students a fortune, many still feel it's easy money. Albert used money from past experiments to purchase books. He used his recent earnings for a trip to California. Jerry, a senior at a large university, has participated in asthma tests since high school, and averages $500 per experiment. "You're getting all of this free medical care," he says. "It has also helped me out on a couple of spring breaks and I have a brand new stereo in my room."

5.   But students also must understand there are potential negatives. Volunteers sometimes experience adverse reactions such as nausea, low blood pressure, or headaches. The more time-consuming tests may also require a hospital stay. Many students are also concerned about parental disapproval or getting labelled by peers as a "lab rat."

6.   Students squeamish about drugs or treatments can try less intrusive research such as questionnaires and taste tests. For students who can't take a vacation from studying, there is always sunscreen testing. "It was great," says Glenda, waterproof sunscreen guinea pig and graduate of a New Jersey university. "I was paid to spend time sitting in a whirlpool and under a sun lamp."

C.   Write ten information questions on the article "Sell Yourself to Science."

D.   Exchange questions with a partner.

E.   Answer your partner's questions.

Write About It

Focus on the Topic Sentence and Supporting Details

Write a four-paragraph composition about how students can stay healthy.

First make an outline with clear topic sentences. For each topic sentence, list at least three supporting details—examples, statistics, facts, or reasons. Then develop your paragraphs.

Grammar Close-Up

Passive Voice

Most sentences are expressed in the active voice. This means that the agent (doer) is also the grammatical subject.

ACTIVE VOICE: Caroline Williams **works** in research at MediLab International.

                         agent (doer)   action (verb)

The passive voice is used to change the focus of a statement. The **result or recipient of the action** is used as the grammatical subject in a passive statement. The form of the verb changes to the past participle with the auxiliary verb used to indicate time.

PASSIVE VOICE: DNA testing **is done** at the laboratory.

                       recipient   action (verb)

For a list of past participles see Appendix 2, page 175.

In a passive sentence, the agent is sometimes mentioned with the expression **by ...**, but it is often not necessary to mention the agent at all.

EXAMPLE: The DNA tests **are supervised by the head technician**.

                Scientific experiments **are conducted** in a lab. (by researchers)

A.   Choose the correct verbs and put them in the **passive voice**.

EXAMPLE: Usually, students who participate in research **are paid**. (pay)

call   study   concern   absorb   advertise   conduct   give
ask   use   recruit

1. Medical studies _____ in the "Help wanted" section of
    student newspapers.

2. Drug companies want to know how well medicine _____.

3. In the first stage, guinea pigs _____ in medical research
    projects.

4. People who take part in tests _____ human guinea pigs.

5. Students _____ to participate in medical experiments.

6. Some students _____ about parental disapproval if they
    participate.

7. Some volunteers _____ to be available during weekends.

8. In one test, volunteers _____ money to sit under sun lamps.

9. Medical research _____ in modern laboratories.

10. New medicines _____ through testing programs.

B.   Match these three columns. Then write sentences in the passive voice.

EXAMPLE: Few people **are harmed** by herbal remedies.

1. **Few people**	need	to freshen breath.
2. Aspirin	test	for clinical research (by drug companies).
3. Tooth decay	**harm**	by oral bacteria.
4. Peppermint gum	prescribe	**by herbal remedies**.
5. New drugs	chew	by doctors.
6. Medicines	prevent	in scientific journals (by researchers).
7. Research reports	cause	on healthy volunteers.
8. Nausea	publish	for headaches.
9. Volunteers	use	by Europeans.
10. Herbal remedies	give	by eating ginger.

C.   Complete the sentences with the correct form of the auxiliary verb **be**. (present tense: **am, is, are,** or past tense: **was, were**)

1. The results _____ published in a medical journal last month.

2. Ginger _____ recognized as a modern treatment for stomach problems.

3. Minor ailments _____ helped by herbal remedies.

4. Medical wisdom _____ found in many texts from ancient societies.

5. Insulin _____ discovered by a Canadian scientist.

6. Many of her ideas _____ taken from the work of other researchers.

7. Some illnesses _____ given strange names by our ancestors.

8. Knowledge from the past _____ ignored in many medical faculties today.

9. I _____ frightened by the possibility of developing a serious disease.

10. Many medical problems _____ related to stress in our daily lives.

UNIT 11

The Earth Matters

Learning Objectives

In this unit you will:

- discuss the environment

- read about the hole in the ozone layer

- listen to an interview about an environmental farm

- learn how to form questions with the perfective aspect and the passive voice

- watch a video about an environmentally friendly house

- write a composition about the environment

It's important to be involved and stand up for what you believe in.

—*Ione Skye*

Non-Stop Talking

In groups of three or four, talk about these questions. Keep talking for 20 minutes. Be prepared to give the class a summary of your group's ideas and information.

1. How important is the environment to you?

2. Do students today feel the same way about the environment as their parents did?

3. What environmental problems do you know about?

4. Who should be working to solve problems in the environment?

5. What is global warming?

6. What is the greenhouse effect?

7. What is the ozone layer?

8. What is the problem with the ozone layer?

9. What kind of health problems can be caused by the thinning ozone layer?

10. What can people do about this problem?

11. What does "environmentally friendly" mean?

12. How can a house be environmentally friendly?

13. How does recycling help the environment?

14. Which things can be recycled?

15. What products can be made from recycled materials?

16. Do you know about any groups that help the environment?

17. What can students do to help the environment?

18. What are some ways to save gas or heating oil?

19. What are some things all individuals can do to help the environment?

20. How do you envision the environment 20 years from now?

Earthship

 VIDEO ACTIVITY 7

Can a house be environmentally friendly? What kind of recycled materials can be used in building a house? Watch the video to find out.

First, read the sentences to prepare for the video. As you watch, complete the sentences.

1. The fluff in Earth Homes helps prevent _____.

2. Pat uses her house to show students that they can

   _____.

3. The house gives people something very powerful: _____.

4. To build the house, they use recycled materials such as

   _____ , scrap _____ ,

   and used _____.

5. They are paid to take _____.

6. Pat, Chuck, and 200 students worked on Earthship for the past

   _____.

7. Pat loves to work with kids because

   _____.

8. Barrett Brown thinks this is a

   _____.

9. They collect scrap materials from

   _____.

10. Barrett is now building _____.

11. Earthship will be finished _____.

12. As Earthkeepers, the Potters want to show kids

    _____.

13. According to Pat, to be the richest person on the planet, you should

    _____.

The World Around Us

Work with a partner to complete the puzzle. If you need help, you can turn to "What's What?," the glossary of environmental terms on page 159.

Across

2. Energy from the sun can be replaced or renewed. It is called _____ energy.

3. A warming of the earth's surface is called the _____ effect.

6. The act of cutting down trees and depleting forests is called _____.

7. Dumping chemicals and waste into oceans, lakes, and rivers causes water _____.

9. _____ is an example of a fossil fuel.

11. Rain mixed with pollutants is called _____ rain.

12. The scientific study of the relationships between living things is called _____.

14. Animals and plants that are in danger of becoming extinct are called _____ species.

15. Things that are capable of being broken down into their basic elements are _____.

16. Food grown without the use of chemical fertilizers, pesticides, or herbicides is called _____ food.

Down

1. Coal and oil cannot be replaced once they are used. They are examples of _____ energy sources.

4. Dangerous chemicals in our environment are called _____ wastes.

5. The principal gas that contributes to the greenhouse effect is _____.

8. A thin layer of gas that protects the earth from ultraviolet radiation is called _____.

10. The _____ is the region where life exists, including soil, water, and the lower atmosphere.

13. Places to dump garbage are called _____.

A Hole in the Heavens

A. Focus on Content

Read the complete article. Then complete the sentences that follow.

A Hole in the Heavens

Calvin Sims

Punta Arenas, Chile—The people of this quiet port city, situated along the Strait of Magellan at the bottom of the world, do not venture outside without first rubbing sunblock over their exposed skin and donning dark glasses. For this practice, the 113,000 residents of Punta Arenas have one man to thank or to despise. He is Bedrich Magas, an electrical engineering professor at the city's University of Magallanes.

It was Mr. Magas who first alerted the people of his hometown to the dangers of a large hole in the ozone layer above Punta Arenas that exposes the area to what he says are unsafe levels of radiation.

For the past eight years, Mr. Magas has appeared on television and radio programs, lectured to community groups, school children and agricultural associations, warning people to avoid prolonged exposure to the sun.

As he walks through the streets of Punta Arenas, whose fair-skinned residents and gabled houses are remi-

niscent of Maine or Nova Scotia, Mr. Magas is often approached by mothers who complain that their children's exposed skin turns bright pink when they play outdoors and farmers who say their sheep are going blind from cataracts they attribute to the sun's rays.

Mr. Magas tells them to shield themselves from the sun during the peak hours of the day and to put pressure on the Government to finance research projects into the impact the radiation may have on them. "It is much too early in the process to say for certain that the problems these people are experiencing are due to ozone depletion," Mr. Magas said, "but what we do know is that such high levels of radiation

are dangerous and they destroy. We are facing a worldwide emergency that is starting in Antarctica and spreading north and something must be done."

Under an international treaty, production of the gases that cause the ozone depletion is being phased out, and the rate at which the gas is accumulating in the atmosphere has declined.

Dora Tranáñez, a store clerk, said she first learned about the ozone hole from a television program featuring Mr. Magas. "God bless him, he's a very good man because he's the only one telling us how to protect ourselves," Ms. Tranáñez said. "I've lived here for more than 30 years and I can feel the sun is much stronger than before."

But not everyone thinks that Mr. Magas is the voice of reason. To many in the scientific and business communities here, Mr. Magas is a Chicken Little, who is irresponsibly frightening residents without any scientific evidence to back up his claims.

The last provincial mayor

here publicly called Mr. Magas an "ecoterrorist" and said he was destroying the lucrative ecological tourist industry that Punta Arenas desperately needs as its sheep industry declines. The city has become the major gateway to the Antarctic, producing jobs related to the cruise ships that call here and the flights that stop here. "Magas is a very smart man but he's running around like crazy scaring people out of their wits," said a prominent local travel agent, who spoke on condition that he not be identified. "There's no reason to be alarmed until there is concrete evidence."

While there are no conclusive studies that show a link between an increase in ultraviolet radiation and strange happenings in Punta Arenas, tales of rabbits so blind that hunters grab them by their ears and rumours of blind salmon caught in Tierra del Fuego are often repeated.

Doctors here said there has been no increase in the rate of skin cancer caused by solar radiation since the ozone hole was detected in 1986, but they note that such

an increase would not be evident for another 20 to 25 years.

What is certain is that Punta Arenas, the world's southernmost city, is the only place on earth where large numbers of people live under a giant hole in the ozone layer. Ozone is a thin layer of gas that protects the earth from damaging ultraviolet radiation.

Scientists believe the ozone hole, which is centred over Antarctica, was caused by the use of chlorofluorocarbons, commonly called CFC's, once used heavily as propellants for aerosols, and now limited mostly to refrigerants and plastic foams. The CFC's destroy ozone, and have created a marked thinning in the layer over the South Pole. The hole expands and contracts, and typically from late August to early December it covers the tip of South America.

Gino Casasa, director of Antarctic programs at the university, said that while he respects his colleague's intentions to raise concerns about ozone depletion, he thinks Mr. Magas is an

alarmist. "Everybody agrees that ozone is a big concern, but the problem I see is that the population doesn't understand that there's no scientific data showing any impact on biological life here," Mr. Casasa said. "People are spreading myths about rabbits and buying expensive eyeglasses and creams without any basis."

Mr. Magas said that he has been pressed by past university presidents not to talk about the ozone hole, since it is not his area of expertise. At one point, he said the university threatened to revoke funding for his research projects if he kept speaking out, but has not followed through.

"Why shouldn't we speak as loudly and as accurately as possible about this problem that will have a tremendous impact on the earth," Mr. Magas said. "I have been careful not to create a panic over the ozone hole, but people are hard-headed and you have to constantly hit them over the head again and again for them to fully realize the ramifications of the situation."

Check **three** correct ways to complete each sentence.

1. When they go outside, the residents of Punta Arenas, Chile
    a) ___ put on sun block.
    b) ___ wear brightly coloured clothes.
    c) ___ put on sun glasses.
    d) ___ stay outside for a long time.
    e) ___ avoid prolonged exposure to the sun.

2. Bedrich Magas
    a) ___ is an electrical engineering professor.
    b) ___ first alerted people to the dangers of the ozone hole.
    c) ___ tries to frighten people about the ozone layer for no reason.
    d) ___ works part time as a travel agent.
    e) ___ appears on television and radio to talk about ozone depletion.

3. Symptoms associated with prolonged sun exposure include
    a) ___ people's skin turning violet.
    b) ___ children's skin turning bright pink.
    c) ___ sheep getting cataracts.
    d) ___ people becoming crazy.
    e) ___ rabbits and salmon going blind.

4. Mr. Magas says
    a) ___ high levels of radiation are dangerous.
    b) ___ we are sure the problems people have are due to the ozone depletion.
    c) ___ we are facing a world-wide emergency.
    d) ___ strange happenings in Punta Arenas are just coincidence.
    e) ___ people should pressure the government to research projects on ozone depletion.

5. People who disagree with Mr. Magas say
    a) ___ Mr. Magas is frightening people irresponsibly.
    b) ___ Mr. Magas has no scientific evidence for his claims.
    c) ___ Mr. Magas is the only one telling the truth.
    d) ___ Mr. Magas is the voice of reason.
    e) ___ there is no reason to be alarmed until there is concrete evidence.

6. Doctors and scientists say
    a) ___ there has been no increase in the rate of skin cancer caused by solar radiation so far.
    b) ___ the ozone hole is caused by the use of CFCs.
    c) ___ the hole in the ozone layer is always the same size.
    d) ___ the ozone layer protects the earth from ultraviolet rays.
    e) ___ an increase in skin cancers would be evident in the next five years.

7. Mr. Magas continues to talk about the ozone layer
    a) ___ even though he was asked by university professors not to talk about it.
    b) ___ because he thinks the problem will not have a big impact.
    c) ___ because people are hard-headed and don't really listen to the warnings.
    d) ___ even though the university threatened to revoke his funding.
    e) ___ because he wants to create panic about the ozone hole.

B. Put It Together

Match the sections to create eight sentences.

A	B	C
Mr. Magas	to revoke funding	turned bright pink.
Mothers complained	a major gateway	that protects the earth.
Dora Tranáñez says	called Mr. Magas	for cruise ships.
The last provincial mayor	a thin layer of gas	the ramifications of the situation.
Puentas Arenas is	people don't realize	for Mr. Magas's research.
The ozone layer is	that only Mr. Magas	an "ecoterrorist."
The university threatened	first alerted people	is telling the truth.
Mr. Magas says	when children's skin	to the dangers of radiation.

1. _____
2. _____
3. _____
4. _____
5. _____
6. _____
7. _____
8. _____

C. Focus on Language

Cross out the word or phrase in each row that doesn't belong.

1.	ozone	UV rays	ecoterrorist	radiation
2.	community	associations	residents	reminiscent
3.	production	thinning	contraction	depletion
4.	studies	evidence	myths	data
5.	panic	rumours	alarm	frightening
6.	damage	destroy	lucrative	danger

Environmental Farm

LISTENING ACTIVITY 11

A. Prepare to Listen

Work in groups to discuss these questions.

1. How much time do you spend outdoors?

2. How can people feel more connected with nature?

3. Did you ever think about getting "back to the land"?

B.   Listen for Information

This listening passage is from "Outfront," a radio program written and produced by teenagers. It's about an environmental farm where students gather to learn about helping the environment and work on the land. You will hear Tegan Wong interview several people. As you listen, make notes about the information you hear.

Tegan Wong:

Age:

Where she grew up:

The biggest things on her mind:

a)

b)

Her father's job:

Her mother's job:

What she studies at university:

Why she came to New Brunswick:

The Fallsbrooke Centre

What it is:

Who set it up:

Leland Doherty

What the song he sings is about:

How he came to Fallsbrooke:

What he brought with him:

How long he's been there:

Conchi

The song she sings at first:

Where she's from:

What she thinks of Fallsbrooke Centre:

What her second song is about:

What happens the next day:

Leland Doherty

What Leland is doing the next day:

Why he uses hand tools:

Jean Arnold

What she likes to do, wherever she goes:

How she sowed seed in her first garden:

What she thinks this shows us:

Tegan Wong

The places she has met people from:

What she's been doing for the last three months:

The downside of butternut seeds:

Where she's going:

How she lived for the last five months:

Grammar Close-Up

Questions With the Perfective Aspect and the Passive Voice

Questions With the Perfective Aspect

The perfective form of verbs can be simple (the **present perfect**) or continuous (the **present perfect continuous**). In both forms, the auxiliary verb **have/has** is used to form negatives and questions.

EXAMPLES: **Have** you **tried** coffee without sugar?

Have you **been waiting** all afternoon?

A.   Make questions in the **present perfect** from the sentences below. Use the question words given.

EXAMPLE: You **have been** somewhere all my life.

   Where **have** you **been** all my life?

1. Sam has done something to upset his girlfriend.

    What _____?

2. You have been somewhere most of the afternoon.

    Where _____?

3. They have contributed to the environment by reducing consumption.

    How _____?

4. Mr. Smith has been an environmentalist forever.

    How long _____?

5. They have opposed building the dam because they felt it was wrong.

    Why _____?

6. Everyone has agreed to demonstrate against the project tomorrow.

    When _____?

7. Demonstrators have marched to the director's office.

    Where _____?

8. People have protested in front of the municipal offices.

    Where _____?

9. The demonstrators have planned this because they believe in it.

    Why _____?

10. We have arranged to meet in the parking lot of the city hall.

    Where _____?

B.   Use the **present perfect continuous** to complete the questions below.

EXAMPLE: What _____ (farmers / growing) for centuries?

   What **have** farmers **been growing** for centuries?

1. Why _____ (people / demonstrate) against building the dam?

2. How long _____ (they / plan) to build this dam in the Amazon?

3. Where _____ (government / meet) to consider what to do about it?

4. What _____ (opponents / think) about doing to stop the project?

5. Since when _____ (people / feel deprived) of their ancestral rights?

6. Who _____ (the government / expect) to support this initiative?

7. What _____ (environmentalists / predict) would happen?

8. Where _____ (the ozone layer / show) signs of weakness?

9. How _____ (citizens / react) to warnings in Punta Arenas?

10. When _____ (scientists / predict) disaster for the environment?

Questions With the Passive Voice

The **passive voice** form of questions makes questions using the verb **be** as the auxiliary verb. The main verb is expressed with the past participle. The auxiliary verb is used to express time (past or present).

EXAMPLES: Where **are** mushrooms **found**?

How **were** the pyramids **build**?

A.   Make questions from the statements below, using the passive voice. Use the present or past tense form of the auxiliary verb.

Scientists **discovered** a hole in the ozone layer.
What was discovered in the ozone layer? (a hole)

1. Punta Arenas is situated on the Strait of Magellan.

   Where _____?

2. People were alerted to the hole in the ozone layer by Mr. Magas's warnings.

   How _____?

3. Mr. Magas was called an ecoterrorist by the mayor of Punta Arenas.

   What _____?

4. Punta Arenas is known as the gate to the Antarctic.

   What _____?

5. We were told some strange stories about blind rabbits.

   What kind of _____?

6. Blind salmon are caught in Tierra del Fuego.

   Where _____?

7. The giant hole in the ozone layer was first detected in 1986.

    When _____?

8. The ozone hole is situated over the continent of Antarctica.

    Where _____?

9. The ozone hole was caused by the use of chlorofluorocarbons.

    How _____?

10. Concerns about the ozone hole are seldom raised at the university.

    Where _____?

Write About It

Focus on Developing Ideas

Write a five-paragraph composition on helping the environment. Use information from the unit, as well as your own ideas. Be sure that each paragraph has a topic sentence and supporting details.

Two Sides to Every Question

Choose one of the following subjects. When the teacher calls your name, talk for one or two minutes to support **Statement A**. When the teacher says "Stop," switch to **Statement B**, and give arguments to support it. The class will decide which of your arguments is most convincing.

1. **Statement A:** Most people don't know much about environmental problems, and don't care about them either.
   Statement B: Many people care about the environment and want to make changes.

2. **Statement A:** The people who built "Earthship" from recycled materials are unique individuals. Not many people would take this sort of action.
   Statement B: Young adults care more about the environment than their parents do, and will learn new ways to save the world.

3. **Statement A:** It's very hard for individuals to have much impact on environmental problems.
   Statement B: Every individual can make a difference in cleaning up the environment.

4. **Statement A:** Problems such as the depleted ozone layer and global warming are probably exaggerated.
   Statement B: People should start doing something about environmental problems before it's too late.

What's What?

A Glossary of Commonly Used Environmental Terms

Acid Rain   Rain mixed with chemicals such as sulphur dioxide and nitrogen oxides, caused by emissions from various sources.

Biodegradable   Capable of being broken down by bacterial processes into basic elements or compounds.

Biosphere   The regions of earth where life can exist, including soil, water, and the lower atmosphere.

Carbon dioxide   A gas produced by industry, chiefly from burning fossil fuels.

Deforestation   The rapid destruction of forests, contributing to the greenhouse effect and the loss of animal and plant species.

Ecology   The scientific study of living things (humans, animals, and plants) in relation to one another and their environment.

Endangered species   Animals and plants that are in danger of becoming extinct.

Fossil fuels   Fuels such as coal, oil, or natural gas formed from fossil remains of ancient plant and animal life.

Greenhouse effect   A phenomenon in which growing amounts of carbon dioxide trap heat in the atmosphere, causing global warming.

Hazardous wastes   Materials that are dangerous to humans, wildlife, and the environment at large and require special disposal techniques.

Landfills   Garbage dumps that are usually pits into which waste is emptied and covered with soil.

Nonrenewable energy sources   Sources that cannot renew themselves or be replaced once they are used. Examples include coal and oil.

Organically grown food   Food grown without use of chemical fertilizers, pesticides, or herbicides.

Ozone   A thin layer of gas formed naturally in the upper atmosphere. The ozone protects the earth from damaging ultraviolet radiation.

Pollution   The act of putting chemicals or sewage into the air or water.

Renewable energy sources   Sources that can renew themselves or be replaced, such as solar energy and wood.

Solar energy   Energy from the sun, a renewable energy source.

Great Performances

Learning Objectives

In this unit you will:

- discuss different kinds of entertainment

- listen to an interview with Sylvie Frechette and the Cirque du Soleil

- read about a student who earns money by busking

- learn about gerunds

- watch a video about creating firework displays

YOUR DAILY SMILE

Happiness is different from pleasure. Happiness has something to do with struggling and enduring and accomplishing.

—*George Sheehan*

Non-Stop Talking

In groups of three or four, talk about these questions. Keep talking for 20 minutes. Be prepared to give the class a summary of your group's ideas and information.

1. What is your favourite kind of entertainment?

2. How often do you go to concerts?

3. How often do you go to plays at the theatre?

4. What was the best show you ever saw?

5. What was the worst show you ever saw?

6. Did you ever perform in a show? Describe your experience.

7. If you could be very talented in one area, which would you choose?

8. Who is your favourite performer?

9. What kinds of movies do you like best?

10. What was the best movie you ever saw?

11. Have you ever been to the Cirque du Soleil?

12. What makes this show different from other circuses?

13. What are some special effects you see in movies or shows?

14. Which movie or show had the most unusual special effects?

15. What kinds of shows do you see in summer festivals?

16. What was the best fireworks display you ever saw? Describe it.

17. If you could choose to perform in any movie or show, which would you like to perform in?

18. Do you ever see street artists in the subway or on a street corner? Describe what they do.

19. How are street performances different from shows in a theatre?

20. Why do you think street performers choose to perform in this way?

"O"

CBC ⬤ LISTENING ACTIVITY 12

Interview with Sylvie Frechette and the Cirque du Soleil

A. Prepare to Listen

Read these paragraphs with a partner. Chose the correct words to complete the information.

Most people (**1.** know, knows, have known) the Cirque du Soleil as a show, with amazing acrobatics and daredevil acts. Now there is a new extravaganza, and it takes place 17 feet (5 metres) underwater, at the bottom of a pool. The pool (**2.** serves, is serving, has served) as a stage for the Cirque's new challenge in Las Vegas.

The show is called "O" (for "eau"), and the performers are (**3.** saturated, saturates, saturate) in it. Computerized equipment (**4.** is suspend, suspended, is suspended) 60 feet (18 metres) above the liquid stage. It lowers and lifts props, scenery, and artists in and out of the water and makes the death-defying flips and gravity-defying leaps even more spectacular. The Cirque (**5.** has always had, have always had, have had always) unique special effects, but now the water is part of the magic.

Sylvie Frechette, Olympic synchronized swimming champion, (**6.** coaches, has coached, is coached) the team of swimmers. She (**7.** is saying, says, was saying) that working in the water presents special challenges. All of the makeup and costumes have to be waterproof. All of the 75 performers had to be trained for underwater work, and many of them (**8.** weren't, wasn't, aren't) used to working wet. Gymnasts had problems because they were unnatural swimmers due to their low body fat and dense muscles. Synchronized swimmers had to learn to be less robotic and precision-oriented. They all had to get used to (**9.** plunges, plunged, plunging) into the water from great heights, (**10.** swimming, swims, was swimming) through visual effects like coloured lights and bubbles, and (**11.** dodging, to dodge, will dodge) underwater platforms. It (**12.** won't be without, going to be, will be without) dangers and challenges, but the final effect is spectacular, and the acrobatics (**13.** stuns, are stunning, are stunned).

B. Listen for Details

As you listen, complete the sentences.

1. Since she was a little girl Sylvie dreamed about _____.

2. There will be _____ seats in the water theatre.

3. The ceiling will be _____ feet high.

4. The water theatre will be permanently in _____.

5. After Atlanta, Sylvie wanted to _____, from synchronized swimming.

6. She will be a _____, a _____, and also an _____.

7. She is in charge of the _____.

8. To do testing in the water, they created _____.

9. Next week she will try to _____ into the water.

10. Now they are using different pools _____.

11. They will rehearse for _____ months in Las Vegas.

12. The aquatic talent has to be very good _____.

13. They test the _____, the _____ and they had to _____ from different heights.

14. They tested to see if they were afraid of _____.

15. They had to jump on a net that was _____ feet high.

16. Now there are _____ people, but it will be cut down to _____ by June.

17. They started with _____ résumés. They cut it down to _____, and after the audition they cut it down to _____.

18. There will be _____ shows a night, _____ nights a week.

19. At the Olympics, athletes train _____ for _____ big moment.

20. Julie Sauvé has been Sylvie's coach for _____ years.

21. Sylvie is happy there will be no rules about _____.

22. The bottom of the pool is divided into four different _____.

23. The pool is _____ feet deep.

24. They can stand at the bottom of the pool for _____ hour.

25. They can do anything they want to, as long as the public is _____.

Busking for Dollars

A. Prepare to Read

This article begins with a dialogue and personal comment. Read this introduction with a partner until you get to **paragraph 1**. Predict what the story is about. Then read the rest of the story, and answer the questions that follow.

BUSKING FOR DOLLARS
Fiona Coll

Police: Excuse me," said the burly policeman. "I'm going to have to ask you to leave."

Fiona: "Oh?" I replied, my voice oozing with all the saccharine innocence I could muster. "May I ask why?"

Police: "Loitering is prohibited in this area."

Fiona: "Sir, I'm not loitering."

Police: "What are you doing, then?"

Fiona: "Entertaining the masses," I grinned. The policeman's face darkened menacingly.

Police: "Really," he replied slowly. I held up my instrument as proof.

Fiona: "I'm providing these passers-by with an aural remedy for the mind-numbing trash noise of the city. A little distraction, if you will, from their busy schedules, their power lunches. Think of me as a public service. Think of the higher productivity I'm promoting, by boosting morale…" I was speaking in my very best earnest-and-committed-idealistic voice. Unfortunately, this voice was also reminiscent of my insolent-and-insubordinate-youth voice, and I had a sneaking suspicion that I was close to crossing the line.

"Isn't freedom of artistic expression a right protected by the constitution of this nation, by the very fabric of our moral countenance?" Suddenly, a brief but powerful mental image of me making one lonely phone call from a small, grey, metal room where floor-to-ceiling bars were standard decor popped into my head.

Police: "I won't ask you again, young lady."

I decided it was probably time to let someone else try their best on that particular street corner. I fled.

And so went one of my first busking experiences a few years ago. I've long been fascinated by the myriad of performers who take to the streets and subways, the malls and urban courtyards, to sing and dance and play and juggle, and ultimately, to entertain.

1. Busking is essentially the act of performing in a public place, for which donations are hopefully made by the transient pedestrian audience. That definition doesn't really cut it, though, because busking has evolved into a subtly complex and sophisticated art form with its own rules, regulations, and culture.

2.   Nowadays, buskers, or street performers, as they're also known, can be musicians, actors, dancers, magicians, jugglers, contortionists, puppeteers, fire eaters, insect tamers—the list goes on. Some would even include sidewalk painters and those people who wrap your hair in little coloured threads as variants on the theme. No matter what the specifics, busking is characterized by a magical closeness between performer and audience—an interaction that isn't found in many other artistic endeavours. There are now busking festivals all over the world, with hundreds of thousands of people visiting to see those unique performances. Skilled buskers pride themselves on never repeating a performance—every different audience, sidewalk, building, even weather condition becomes an integral part of the show.

3.   So, what sort of people are these buskers, you ask? Ah, I reply. Now the fun begins. It takes talent and intrepidity to step up and capture a crowd that doesn't belong to you. These are not regular shows on proper stages, where people buy tickets, then sit down to watch and listen. Busking audiences are drawn from people on their way to other places, wandering around with other things on their collective minds. Buskers must be dynamic and compelling enough to attract attention to themselves, and fearless enough to venture boldly into weird and not-necessarily-wonderful environments. Spontaneity is another must, but perhaps the most outstanding characteristic of successful street performers is their bloody-minded dedication to their craft and perseverance in the face of considerable adversity.

4.   For busking has yet to be fully accepted as a legitimate enterprise by many of society's dark forces. Cities have long tried to ban, tax, discourage, and control street performers. Buskers are continually having their equipment confiscated or being thrown in jail for various "crimes," including loitering, panhandling, and infraction of noise bylaws. Here's where things get a little tricky. How should a healthy busking scene be maintained? Shopkeepers need to keep their doorways clear for people to use, and pedestrians need the sidewalk. But a majority of buskers are sensitive to their surroundings, and can do their thing without compromising public space. The fact remains that busking is commonly regarded as a suspicious activity and those wielding the power of the law are commonly quick to use it when it comes to shutting down the sidewalk shows.

5.   Still, in an oddly ironic twist, it appears that adversity and opposition have bred first class, sharp-as-the-knives-they-toss performers. It's good to see the growth of busking festivals all around the world and a little recognition and reward is in order. Festivals are held coast to coast in North America, as well as across Europe and in Australia and New Zealand. Many buskers make their living by following the circuit across the globe—a meagre living, if you're counting dollars and cents, but what it lacks in financial security, it makes up for in bizarre life experience. The festivals are gaining in both size and fame. The Halifax International Busker Festival boasted an attendance of over half a million people at their 1993 event.

6.   I met some real live street performers in my travels this summer. Take Eva Festa, as an example. Eva came up to talk to me as I played on a corner in Ireland. She was from San Francisco, but living in Ireland on the money she made on the festival circuit in New Zealand. I was impressed.

Fiona: "What do you do?"

Eva: "I have a one-woman show," she answered. "I write music for voice and violin. I perform it myself."

Fiona: Wow, I thought. She can sing and play at the same time. Silly me. But she wasn't finished yet.

Eva: "...and I do it on a trapeze."

7.   That's about when I started choking. I promptly bought both her albums, and they were good. Ireland is filled with musical buskers—instruments of all sizes and shapes, and people from all walks of life. One day I came across a guy who was putting on a puppet show, complete with live soundtrack, all by himself. He had instruments and attachments hooked up to every available limb and even then I don't know how he did it.

8.   Then I visited Edinburgh, Scotland, home of 473 billion festivals. The streets were literally lined with performers. There were gospel choirs, fiddle players, theatre troupes, clowns, mimes. There were a group of silent body sculptors, who made all sorts of odd shapes and scenes using only each other for support. I saw a man on stilts, painted entirely silver, who would stand absolutely still for minutes, then strike another pose and freeze again. I had to watch him for a while, just to make sure he wasn't a figment of my imagination. Every city, no matter how culturally renowned, seems to have a contingent of buskers somewhere. If you live in say, Calgary, Canada, where the temperature is currently –87 degrees C, the busking season is somewhat limited to the summer months. (Mmmm, summer...) But have a look around—you may be surprised at what you find.

B. Focus on Content

Answer these questions with a partner.

1. Write a definition of busking, using information in paragraph 1. Put the definition into your own words.

   _____

   _____

2. Find ten examples of types of street performers from paragraph 2.

   a) _____   e) _____   h) _____

   b) _____   f) _____   i) _____

   c) _____   g) _____   j) _____

   d) _____

3. What two things make busking different from performing on a stage? (paragraph 2)

   _____

   _____

4. How is busking regarded by many people? Give examples of how buskers have been treated from paragraph 4.

   _____

   _____

5. How does the author feel about her experience as a busker? Write one or two sentences to summarize her point of view.

   _____

   _____

C. Focus on Language

Answer these questions with a partner.

1. The author uses a mixture of styles, including dialogue, narration, and exposition. Why do you think she does this?

2. At the end of the first dialogue, the author has an image of making a phone call from a "small, grey, metal room where floor-to-ceiling bars are standard decor." What is this room?

   _____

3. The author uses several hyphenated terms to describe things. Match the expressions to the words with similar meaning.

   a) earnest-and-committed-idealist voice ____   1. flashy

   b) insolent-and-insubordinate-youth voice ____   2. bad places to be

   c) not-necessarily-wonderful environments ____   3. sincere

   d) sharp-as-the-knives-they-toss performers ____   4. provocative

4. In paragraph 3, the author uses many words to describe buskers. Find eight words the author uses.

a) _____   e) _____

b) _____   f) _____

c) _____   g) _____

d) _____   h) _____

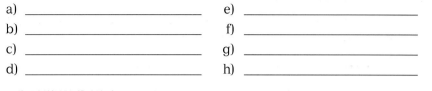

Grammar Close-Up

Gerunds

A gerund is made from a verb, but it functions as a noun. A gerund can function as the subject or object of a sentence. It can also function as the object of a preposition.

EXAMPLES: *Subject:* **Swimming** is good for you.

Object: We like **swimming**.

Object of a preposition: He is interested in **swimming**.

A gerund is made with the present participle form of the verb (ing form without the auxiliary verb be). Look at the examples of a noun and a gerund.

EXAMPLES: *Noun:* **Plays** are exciting.

Gerund: **Performing** in a play is exciting.

The verb **go** + gerund is often used to describe sports and activities. Examples include **go camping, go skiing, go dancing, go jogging, go shopping**.

A. Underline the subject in each sentence. Match the subjects to the gerunds.

1. Books give interesting information. *d*   a) lying down
2. Exercise is good for people. *e*   b) drawing
3. Humour makes people laugh. *i*   c) swimming
4. Cigarettes are dangerous to your health. *h*   d) reading
5. Weights build strong muscles. *e*   e) body building
6. Silence is golden. *g*   f) dancing
7. Ballet develops the muscles. *f*   g) keeping quiet
8. Art develops the mind. *b*   h) smoking
9. Rest helps relax the body. *a*   i) telling jokes
10. TV can be educational for children. *j*   j) watching TV

B.   Replace the noun **something** with the gerund form of one of the verbs above.

perform   rehearse   play   dive   rent   visit   watch   dance
provide   coach

1. **Something** music is an enjoyable pastime.
2. **Something** a video is cheaper than going to a movie.
3. To be a champion swimmer, you need a lot of **something**.
4. **Something** in public takes a lot of courage and talent.
5. **Something** a new city is exciting and interesting.
6. **Something** street performers is amusing.
7. **Something** into the water from a trapeze can be challenging.
8. Many street festivals involve **something** and singing.
9. Before a performance, **something** is very important.
10. **Something** passers-by with a street performance can be a public service.

Gerunds Following Prepositions

A.   Circle the prepositions. Then complete the sentences with the gerund form of the verbs below.

say   swim   watch   forget   buy   drive   write   go   bring   see

1. Susan is afraid of _____ in the deep end of the pool.
2. They are tired of _____ sitcoms on TV.
3. We should thank Bob for _____ us to the show.
4. Max is really good at _____ music.
5. Jenna is worried about _____ her lines in the play.
6. Is anyone interested in _____ the fireworks display tonight?
7. Everyone is excited about _____ to the concert on Saturday.
8. Did you think about _____ your binoculars to the opera?
9. Let's not leave without _____ goodbye.
10. Don't go to the show without _____ tickets in advance.

B.   Complete the sentences with the correct prepositions before the gerunds.

from   to   of   about   for   before   at   in   after   over

1. Let's have coffee _____ **going** to the musical.
2. Are you interested _____ **seeing** a movie on Friday?
3. How _____ **going** for dinner after the show?

4. We are thinking ___of___ **inviting** Annie to join us.

5. Thank you very much ___for___ **attending** my show.

6. Marc is pretty good ___at___ **playing** the piano.

7. We are looking forward ___to___ **hearing** the concert.

8. We can go to the theatre ___after___ **parking** the car.

9. We are tired ___from___ **rehearsing** all day.

10. They chose the concert ___over___ **going** to a movie.

Fireworks

VIDEO ACTIVITY 8

Every summer, people gather outdoors to watch fireworks displays, the spectacular shows that light up on the sky with exploding chrysanthemums. This video is about people who create fireworks displays, and the way they design their shows.

First, read the sentences below. Then, as you watch the video, complete the information.

1. Paul is one of Manitoba's top _____.

2. The event is _____.

3. Paul became hooked on fireworks when his mother told him not to _____.

4. He has staged over _____ shows.

5. The size of the bombs are _____ inches to _____ inches.

6. The bomb goes _____ feet in the air.

7. The "big daddy" is _____ inches, weighs _____ pounds and goes _____ feet in the air.

8. To shoot the bomb, the motion is to _____ and turn back.

9. There are _____ seconds before the bomb goes off.

10. You shouldn't look back to see if the bomb went off because _____.

11. _____ people gather to see the fireworks.

12. The Roman Candle is used to _____.

13. The five-inch bombs are for _____.

14. Peter is worried about the _____ on the ground.

15. Paul and the bomb jockeys were celebrating a _____.

16. Peter was celebrating _____.

Appendix 1
Spelling

Spelling Verb Forms Ending "ing"

The spelling rules for continuous verbs are different from the rules for regular past tense verbs. For example, with the verb **try**, the past tense is **tried**, but the continuous tense is **trying**.

Rule 1   Verbs that end with **e** drop the **e** and add **ing**:

write   writing

Rule 2   Verbs that end with two consonants (**n,d,k**, **b**, etc.) or with two vowels (**a,e,i,o,u**) add **ing**:

try   trying
read   reading

Rule 3   Verbs that end with a vowel and a consonant double the final letter and add **ing**:

put   putting
Exceptions: consonants **w**, **x**, and **y** (**buy**   **buying**)

Note: Verbs that end **ie** change the **i** to **y** and add **ing**:

die   dying
lie   lying

Spelling Simple Past Tense

2 consonants	add **ed**	work	work**ed**
2 vowels + consonant	add **ed**	need	need**ed**
vowel + **y**	add **ed**	play	play**ed**
consonant + **y**	change **y** to **i** add **ed**	try	tri**ed**
vowel + consonant	double consonant add **ed**	plan	plan**ned**

Not all verbs that end in vowel + consonant double the final letter. Common exceptions are **listened**, **opened**, **answered**.

Spelling Rules with Comparative Forms

Adjectives that end in **y** change **y** to **i** and add **er** for the comparative or **est** for the superlative form:

happy	happier
silly	silliest

Adjectives that end in vowel + consonant double the final letter and add **er** for the comparative or **est** for the superlative form:

fat	fatter
thin	thinner

Spelling Plural Nouns

Nouns that end in **s**, **ch**, **sh**, **z**, **o** add **es** to form the plural:

watch	watches
box	boxes
potato	potatoes

Nouns that end in consonant + **y** change the **y** to **i** and add **es** for the plural form:

city	cities
activity	activities

Nouns that end in vowel + **y** add s:

day	days
key	keys

Nouns that end in **f** or **fe** change the **f** to **v** and add **es** to form the plural:

leaf	leaves
knife	knives

Irregular Plurals

person	people
child	children
woman	women
man	men
mouse	mice
foot	feet
tooth	teeth
ox	oxen

Appendix 2
Past Participles

Many past participles are the same as the regular or irregular past tense forms. Irregular past participles are shown in bold type below.

Present	Past	Past Participle
arise	arose	**arisen**
awake	awoke	**awoken**
be	was, were	**been**
beat	beat	**beaten**
become	became	**become**
begin	began	**begun**
bite	bit	**bitten**
bleed	bled	bled
blow	blew	**blown**
break	broke	**broken**
bring	brought	brought
build	built	built
buy	bought	bought
catch	caught	caught
choose	chose	**chosen**
come	came	**come**
cost	cost	cost
cut	cut	cut
dig	dug	dug
do	did	**done**
draw	drew	**drawn**
drink	drank	**drunk**
drive	drove	**driven**
eat	ate	**eaten**
fall	fell	**fallen**
feed	fed	fed
feel	felt	felt
find	found	found
fly	flew	**flown**
forbid	forbade	**forbidden**
forget	forgot	**forgotten**

forgive	forgave	**forgiven**
freeze	froze	**frozen**
get	got	**gotten** (got)
give	gave	**given**
go	went	**gone**
grow	grew	**grown**
have	had	had
hear	heard	heard
hide	hid	**hidden**
hit	hit	hit
hold	held	held
hurt	hurt	hurt
keep	kept	kept
know	knew	**known**
lay	laid	laid
lead	led	led
leave	left	left
let	let	let
lie	lay	**lain**
lose	lost	lost
make	made	made
mean	meant	meant
meet	met	met
pay	paid	paid
put	put	put
read	read	read
ride	rode	**ridden**
ring	rang	**rung**
rise	rose	**risen**
run	ran	**run**
see	saw	**seen**
sell	sold	sold
send	sent	sent
shake	shook	**shaken**
shine	shone	shone
shoot	shot	shot
show	showed	shown
shrink	shrank	**shrunk**
shut	shut	shut
sing	sang	**sung**
sit	sat	sat
sleep	slept	slept
speak	spoke	**spoken**
spread	spread	spread
spring	sprang	**sprung**
stand	stood	stood

steal	stole	**stolen**
stink	stank	**stunk**
swear	swore	**sworn**
swim	swam	**swum**
take	took	taken
teach	taught	taught
tear	tore	**torn**
tell	told	told
think	thought	thought
throw	threw	**thrown**
understand	understood	understood
wake	woke	**woken**
wear	wore	**worn**
win	won	won
write	wrote	**written**

Credits

The authors would like to acknowledge, with thanks, the copyright holders who gave permission to reprint the following materials.

Articles

"You're Smarter Than You Think" adapted from an article in *Modern Woman* magazine. Reprinted by permission of the author.

"Minimum Wage Hell" reprinted by permission of "Spank! Youth Culture Online," www.spankmag.com.

"The Last Call Is a Close Call" reprinted by permission of Warren Perley, Ponctuation Grafix.

"Midnight Basketball" reprinted by permission of the *Globe and Mail*.

"Hoopla Over Hemp" reprinted by permission of the author.

"Changing the World at 15" reprinted by permission of the author.

"A Matter of Compassion" reprinted by permission of the author and Southam News.

"The Thrill of Risk" Copyright © 1998 by The New York Times. Reprinted by permission.

"Trashing the Fashionphiles" reprinted by permission of the author.

"Get Thee Back, Plastic" reprinted by permission of *Sassy* magazine.

"Cyberlove and Other Catastrophes" reprinted by permission of "Spank! Youth Culture Online," www.spankmag.com.

"This Story Is Rated PG" reprinted by permission of *The Gazette* (Montreal).

"Healing Herbs" reprinted from *The Healing Herbs* ©1991 by Michael Castleman. Permission granted by Rodale Press, Inc.; Emmaus, PA 18098.

"Sell Yourself to Science" from "For students, these lab tests pay" by Laura Petrecca. Copyright 1995, USA TODAY. Reprinted by permission.

"A Hole in the Heavens" Copyright © 1995 by the New York Times Company. Reprinted by permission.

"Busking for Dollars" reprinted by permission of "Spank! Youth Culture Online," www.spankmag.com.

Photographs

Cover image: Air Travel-Plane-Abstract. Pierre-Yves Goavec/Imagebank. **Page 7:** The Slide Farm/Al Harvey. **Page 17:** The Slide Farm/Al Harvey. **Page 24:** Dick Hemingway. **Page 33:** Dick Hemingway. **Page 36:** Canapress/Maclean's/Phill Snel. **Page 42:** Canapress/AP Photo/Luca Bruno. **Page 46:** The Toronto Star/Martin. **Page 49:** The Toronto Star/P. Power.

Page 57: Canapress/Moe Doiron. **Page 71** (top left and right): Dick Hemingway. **Page 71** (bottom) The Slide Farm/Al Harvey. **Page 84**: Canapress/Kamloops Daily News/Murray Mitchell. **Page 88**: Canapress/AP Photo/Alastair Grant. **Page 104**: Dick Hemingway. **Page 110**: Tony Stone Images/Tony Wacker. **Page 120**: Dick Hemingway. **Page 135**: Valan Photos/James R. Page. **Page 139**: Valan Photos/Herman H. Giethoorn. **Page 140**: The Slide Farm/Al Harvey. **Page 146**: Dick Hemingway. **Page 163**: Canapress/Paul Chiasson. **Page 166**: The Slide Farm/Al Harvey.